A
JOURNEY
THROUGH

GRIEF

BEVERLY C. SIMMONS

Chrysalis
BALM AND BLADE PUBLISHING

ISBN: 978-0-9841386-9-2

Published by Chrysalis / Balm and Blade Publishing
1927 Mountain Road
Hamburg, PA 19526
www.balmandblade.com

Cover art by Danussa and GoodStudio
Cover design by T. Jason Vanderlaan

Contents

"As a wife and mother, a church musician, a woman of faith, and a widow at the age of 57, Beverly Simmons weaves together threads of grief, loss, hope, trust, and faithfulness in God's presence, strength, and purpose for our lives. This book is a series of meditations in which Beverly invites us to enter into her journey through the pain and loss of her husband into a new way of being as a strong, single woman with a deep faith in the healing power of God." (The Rev. Jean Campbell)

"As a widow, I can say this book relates! As a reader, you know what the author describes is what a woman goes through after the death of her spouse. She works through loneliness, financial difficulties, parenting a child who is also grieving, and day-to-day struggles as a single person in the struggle to recover and move on in life. It is an easy read and inspiring!" (S. Cram, Director, New Beginnings Grief Ministry)

Preface

After living and ministering on Long Island for 24 years, my husband Jeff took a job in Peekskill, New York. After the move, I found my "dream job" as a church musician at Zion Episcopal Church in Wappingers Falls, New York. The commute from Peekskill took about 45 minutes. We were settling into our new roles (my husband as retreat leader and spiritual director) and looking to spending the next 10-15 years there until we retired. We were even talking about the traveling we wanted to do when that time came.

A year and half later, we were blind-sided with Jeff's diagnosis of colon cancer. Still, we assumed and prayed that he would be healed. After all, he was only 55. It was only three weeks before his death and three weeks after turning 56 (after returning from our son's wedding in Delaware) that his oncologist finally said there was nothing more to do. I notified our son, who was stationed in Japan with the Air Force, but was currently in Australia on his honeymoon. I still couldn't (or wouldn't) wrap my head around the fact that Jeff would soon be gone. We weren't in denial and had talked about what I would do once he was gone. But talking about it and experiencing it are very different, as I was soon to find out.

As I began the journey of widowhood, I also began writing down my experiences and feelings. For those who have already been there, you will recognize much of what I went through. For those who have not yet been there, know that when it happens, you are not alone.

The Moment of Graduation

"His blood pressure is 80 over zero."

The hospice nurse has stopped in to check on my husband, Jeff, who lies in the hospital bed in the living room. For the past 24 hours he has been unresponsive when I speak to him or hold his hand. Although his eyes are open some of the time, I'm not sure he is really seeing. I stand on one side of the bed, his brother on the other.

So what does a blood pressure of 80 over zero mean? The nurse explains that he could die within a few hours or possibly not for a few more days. Some people are just so reluctant to give up that their reserves keep them going even at this point.

Jeff and I have had many conversations over the past months and especially the last few weeks since the doctor told him the chemo was not doing any good and we should get hospice care. Although ready to go and be with Lord, he has been reluctant to leave me.

It was a long road during the last seven months for each of us to reach this point of acceptance. He has been kept comfortable with drugs as necessary and has no fear of dying. I am prepared – or am I? How do you ever say good-bye to your very best friend and your loving husband of 31 years?

And yet I don't want him to linger. We have both been in agreement on that. Ever since the diagnosis of colon cancer that was already in the liver, we have agreed that we would fight this thing as hard as we could, but when it was obvious that there was nothing more that could be done, we would pray for a speedy death. So, three weeks ago today when the doctor informed us that we had reached that point, we put out the word to our friends. We asked them to pray for a holy and peaceful death as quickly as possible.

I spend the morning at my desk only a few feet from the bed so I can watch for any change. Today is the Friday before Palm Sunday. I told him earlier in the week when he could still understand and laugh that I thought he, as a priest who is married to a church musician, ought to know better than to die during Holy Week. I have seven services to play from now through Easter, plus a choir rehearsal before each service and an extra one during the week. Our Rector is very understanding and knows I may not be able to do some or even all of these liturgies. But there is no back up plan and I don't want to leave the parish without music if I can help it.

So I sit at my desk going over the details of the funeral service which we planned together. It will have to be on a Saturday so that many of our friends will be able to drive the two and a half hours from Long Island to get to our parish in Wappingers Falls, NY. Jeff served in a parish in Port Jefferson, Long Island for 22 ½ years and we left only two years ago. Since the nurse is sure he will be dead within a few hours or at most a day or two that will mean a funeral on Holy Saturday. Is that possible?

I call our priest, who assures me that it is. Next I call the Suffragan Bishop of Long Island with whom Jeff spoke about ten days ago. I'll never forget listening in on that phone call when Jeff calmly told him that he was dying and asked if he would be willing to celebrate his funeral. So I check that he would be available that day and promise to get back to him. Next comes a call to the Bishop of Albany to see if he can preach. Yes, he, too, is available then. Two bishops who are both available that day – that's a miracle in itself.

Enough phone calls. I go back to the bed and hold Jeff's hand. I talk to him and tell him that I love him and that he is free to go when it is time. I assure him, with more courage than I feel, that I will be all right. I love him very, very much but when God calls him home, I don't want him to hesitate. I get no response, not even a squeeze of the hand.

One of our cats, Dugal, is curled up by his feet. A few days ago, when I tried to move him off the bed, thinking it was bothering Jeff, he was emphatic that it was fine. So I leave Dugal in place. He definitely senses something is wrong and wants to be there.

Jeff's brother Steve and I eat lunch and after the home health aide arrives, we both go upstairs for a nap. I doubt that either of us slept, but it did feel good to lie down for a bit. The aide had instructions to call if anything changed.

When I came down a couple of hours later Steve was singing hymns to Jeff. I joined in on a couple and then let them have some time alone. At about 4:30 p.m. Steve pointed out that he thought Jeff's breathing was really slowing down. At first, I couldn't tell, but then it became obvious.

As Jeff was taking his last breath at 5 p.m., I called our priest to come. The three of us gathered around the bed and said the prayers for the dying and departed. After he finished, we each turned away and began to cry. Jeff had graduated to eternal life. Such a beautiful life; such a holy death. And at 56, much too young!

The Funeral

Now that Jeff has graduated, how do I pray. I spent the last seven months in intense supplication for his healing. For whatever reason, that prayer was not answered in the way we had both hoped. And yet I had told our priest many months ago that however this ended, I was convinced that God would do the most loving thing possible for each of us. I still believe that. In fact, I have a vivid memory of climbing into bed the night Jeff died and saying, "Lord, I love you. Help me to love you more." This has been one of my arrow prayers for many years.

Even as my heart is breaking with grief, I know that I want and need to stay close to God. He will be my strength to get me through this. Right now, it's hard to see more than one day at a time. It's all I can do to think about what needs to be done today. I'm so thankful to be the minister of music at our parish. At a time like this I want to get as close to God as I can and that means spending time in His presence. And with all of those Holy Week services to play, I'll be in church a lot this week. That is a blessing.

When I arrive for the Palm Sunday service my choir doesn't quite know how to react to me. They have all heard of Jeff's death only two days before and they want to hug me and cry with me. But if I am going to get through this important service that will have to wait. So I ask them please not to give me their condolences until after the service. Otherwise, none of us will be able to play or sing. Somehow, we all get through it. Then I hug and cry with them.

The rehearsal on Wednesday and the service on Maundy Thursday go smoothly. Jeff's visitation hours are in the Parish Hall on Good Friday both before and after the evening Good Friday Liturgy. So I go from one to the other, warming up the choir, playing for the liturgy and then back to the visitation. Yes, the church is where I need to be this week. My consolation comes from doing the work I love, being in God's house, and receiving the Eucharist. There is literally no place I would rather be.

Holy Saturday dawns a beautiful day in late March. As we gather for the funeral I am pleased to see so many people who made the trip from Long Island, New York City, Boston, Michigan and other places. Jeff used to quip that if you want a big funeral you have to die young. I just wish he hadn't decided to prove it!

The liturgy was everything we had both wanted it to be. The church was decorated for Easter and full of people. The hymns were glorious and the liturgy full of hope. It made the Easter Vigil that night seem drab by comparison. My new daughter-in-law carried the Pascal Candle in the procession and my son read a lesson and was a pallbearer. God sustained me through it all with only a few tears during one of the communion hymns. Of course, I knew that if I lost it, the choir would too, so I was trying very hard to keep my composure. But when I followed the casket out of the church and watched them put it in the hearse, I did lose it. Matt came quickly to my side after he helped the other pallbearers and I cried that we have lost a great treasure. How true.

A year and a half after that liturgy, many people still talk about it. It gave them a glimpse of what heaven is like. And more than one person remarked that seeing me carry the Eucharistic elements forward at the Offertory while singing "For all the saints" helped them realize that I am going to be ok. At that point I sure didn't feel like it, even though in my head I knew they were right. God gives us special graces to get through such moments.

The Business of Death

There is much that needs doing in the first few weeks and even months after a death. In some ways this is merciful in that it doesn't allow you to just collapse in grief. Even after all the arrangements for the funeral are taken care of, there are many calls to make.

I called Social Security to report the death and found out while talking with them that Jeff had no income listed for the year 1990. That will impact my future income unless I can find the paperwork to prove his earnings. Luckily, I found our income tax return and was able to get that corrected.

Since we were living at the Convent where my husband was the Chaplain and Director of the Spiritual Life center, his employer knew immediately. And that means the end of any paychecks. So then I had to notify the Church Pension Fund so they could start the process of sending me a monthly pension check.

There were several life insurance companies and groups to notify. And, of course, they all needed a copy of the death certificate. Decisions had to be made about leaving the money invested with them or getting a payout.

Banks and credit cards have to be notified. Most credit card companies either said they would switch the account to my name or else they said I would have 30 days to fill out a form they would send with additional information. But one major company announced that my account would be closed immediately. If I wanted, I could reapply for a card. It seemed like a slap in the face. I didn't think much of their lack of compassion. We had both been on the account and had been very good customers (translation: we had spent lots of money in their stores) for many years.

In addition to the business end, there is also the personal. Lots and lots of thank-you notes had to be written. There were all the people who brought food, those who sent plants or flowers, and thank-you notes for Mass cards. The 3 charities that Jeff had asked people to donate to kept sending me the names of the donors, so that required more thank-you cards. That continued for several months.

Once I had some idea of my new income, I had to make a budget. My husband's pension was down to two-fifths of what his salary had been. On top of that, I was suddenly responsible for paying all of my health insurance. That had always been part of his benefit package. Then there was housing. We lived in a house owned by the Convent with all our utilities paid. The Sisters generously said I could stay on for a year if needed. But clearly, I would have to soon figure out a way to pay for housing. I had a long talk with our financial advisor to try and figure out what I could afford to pay for a house when I started looking.

Those are a lot of decisions to make in the best of times and this was certainly the worst of times. The advice of not making major decisions for a year following the death of a spouse is definitely sound. Unfortunately, in my case I couldn't wait that long. Jeff and I had discussed what I would do long before he died. So I knew I would have to start looking for housing sooner rather than later.

My son was with me for 3 weeks following the funeral and we took our first look at real estate during that time just to get a feel for what was out there and what it cost. Everyone at my parish knew that I wanted to move closer to the church, so they began looking for me. One woman came to me just three months after Jeff's death and said she had a neighbor who would be putting her house on the market soon. She thought it might be a good one for me. I followed her home to see the neighborhood, met the neighbor, and saw the house. It was indeed what I was looking for. The owner agreed to let me know the price before putting it on the market. It was at the top of my price range but we came to an agreement without a realtor (saving us both money) and just six months after Jeff's death, I bought a house! Whew!

Groceries

I had never appreciated the custom of bringing casseroles and other food to the home of a family when they experienced the loss of a loved one. Now I do. What a blessing it was not to have to plan meals! When people in my choir asked about bringing food my first reaction was to say it wasn't necessary. Then I began to realize that not only would my son and daughter-in-law be arriving from Japan, but also my brother from Oregon and my son's in-laws. They were going to be with us for several days. And all of this during Holy Week when I would be running back and forth to church. At that time, I lived a 45-minute drive from Zion Church.

So I called one of my choir members and told her to pass the word that I would appreciate food after all. For the next ten days I hardly had to think about what to put on the table at mealtime.

But the day did eventually come when I had to go grocery shopping. Immediately, I was confronted with my new situation. It isn't as simple as buying half of what I did before. Many items aren't packaged for a single person. Some items I could freeze half for a later date. Other items, if I bought them, I would probably end up either eating more than I really wanted or tossing out some of it when it spoiled.

As I went down the aisles, I began to load my cart with the items I always bought. Then, as I reached for the sardines, it suddenly hit me. I don't like sardines. I bought them for Jeff. So now I will no longer buy them. It seemed that every other item had some memory attached. I found myself crying my way through the store. Is this what life will always be like.

Perhaps the most difficult time of day for me, once all the company had left and I was truly alone, was the dinner hour. Jeff and I had always made time to eat together. It was a high priority in our marriage. It was the time when we could share the joys and frustrations of the day or talk about anything that was coming up. We treasured that time and seldom let anything interfere with it. Now I had to prepare a small dinner and sit down by myself to eat. For a number of weeks, I would sit down to eat and start crying instead. I somehow managed to get the nourishment I needed, but I began to dread that time of day. I would get a knot in the pit of my stomach. I found it hard to face. Somehow, after a number of weeks, it began to subside and I found I could get through the dinner hour more peacefully. But it took time.

How Can I Possibly Pray?

In the aftermath of a death there is so much happening that sitting down in a quiet place to pray is not an option – at least it wasn't for me. Oh, I did plenty of praying all right. But it was either the formal prayers of the Holy Week liturgies or it was the arrow prayers that come from the gut at a time like this: "Lord, have mercy," or "Help me, Lord," or "Jesus, be with me."

Within a few days I knew that I wanted and needed to get into a more purposeful routine of prayer, so I decided to begin by praying the bedtime office of Compline from our Prayer Book. Jeff and I used to like to do this when we were on a camping trip. We'd climb into our sleeping bags, lie on our backs, shine the flashlight on the little booklet and pray together. It takes about five minutes. So I would climb into bed and the last thing before turning the light out, I would pray Compline. It is a wonderful way to calm yourself down just before sleeping and it turns your attention away from everything else and focuses on God. I have continued this practice to the present. When I turn the light out I remain in God's presence and offer my prayers until I fall asleep.

I also discovered that when I awoke in the night for any reason it was a good time to keep focused on God with a few arrow prayers like the one I mentioned I used the night Jeff died: "I love you Lord, help me to love you more." I also use it as a time of offering myself to God for His service.

But all this didn't change the fact that I still wasn't able to get back into my routine of quiet prayer. (In fact, this didn't happen for me for almost eight months.) So when my company left, I returned to the routine that Jeff and I had had from the time of our engagement up to the day he died: I said Morning Prayer each day before going out to start the day's activities. It gave me a structure for prayer when I was unable to sit quietly in God's presence. It kept me connected. I was reading Scripture which nourished me and using the ancient and modern prayers of the church to speak for me.

Although we had been very faithful about praying Morning Prayer, we seldom used Evening Prayer. It seems our schedules made this too difficult. But now I had lots more time and the dinner hour was a difficult time for me. So why not add Evening Prayer before I start preparing dinner? I decided I liked the structure of praying this other office from the Prayer Book. Morning and Evening Prayer are prayed in our Parish Church every day although I am seldom there at those times. At home I pray all the offices out loud. It helps me focus on what I'm saying.

When you break a routine, it can be difficult to start again. I think that was true for me regarding my previous times of quiet prayer. But about eight months after Jeff's death, when I went to see my spiritual director she nudged and encouraged me to start my quiet time again. I did so out of obedience, at first, more than a desire to pray. The first few weeks were a struggle with distractions and feelings like "this isn't working." However, I persevered and am grateful I did. The routine has now been firmly reestablished and has, at times, brought me tremendous joy and blessings. God is always faithful and is just waiting for us to respond.

Sometime during those first few weeks, I remember praying that God would use this experience of grief that I was going through to help someone else someday. I knew I wouldn't be ready for that for quite a while, but I asked Him, when I had come through it, to let me be of service to others who were going through similar circumstances. Little did I know that only 13 months later I would be in exactly that position with one of my very closest friends whose husband was also a priest!

Memories: A Blessing Or A Curse?

Shortly after Jeff's death, I found it very difficult to try to think of him. My memory of him at that point was all wrapped up in the last few months, days, and weeks. I would see him in the hospital dehydrated from the chemo or I would picture him sitting in his recliner during the last week of his life. I saw him trying to use the computer at which he had been a whiz but was now reduced to not knowing how to turn it on. And finally, I would see him during the visiting hours, lying in the coffin vested in the liturgical garments of his ordination which I had so lovingly made for him almost 30 years ago. These were all true memories but not very consoling ones.

Looking around our house I began to notice the photograph gallery which we had completed only a few months before. These pictures began to help me recapture other memories. Here I could remember the choir trip to Spain, our sabbatical in Alaska when we backpacked into Denali Park and camped for two nights surrounded by several grizzly bear families. Photos of our two mission trips to Nepal brought back many wonderful memories. And scattered throughout the collection are pictures of Jeff portaging our canoe, a favorite campsite on a lake in Algonquin Park, Ontario, our son Matt on various camping trips through the years. Here were many happy memories.

So I had a decision to make: either I could cling to the unpleasant memories of the past few months or I could choose to remember all the wonderful times from the past 31 years. I have known widows and widowers who got stuck remembering only the pain and bereavement of the immediate past. The only way they can remember their spouse is with sadness. I didn't want that. I also knew Jeff wouldn't want that for me. We had too much fun and too many wonderful experiences together during those 31 years. So I made a conscious effort to thank God for each unique experience that we had. I would dwell on a particular trip or event and let it play in my mind until I could enjoy it all over again.

As time went on, I noticed something interesting. I had not forgotten the final few months, but they no longer hurt quite as much. I could now see the last weeks of Jeff's life in a more realistic way. They were only one small part of a very wonderful life that we had together. And when pictures from those last weeks would surface, they no longer held the same sting that they had originally. I was able to be thankful for all the little blessings even in those difficult times.

Jeff had prayed when he first got the diagnosis that whatever the outcome, he wanted to glorify God and continue to serve Him. So I remembered when the social workers from Hospice came to talk with us just two weeks before his death. They are obviously well-trained to help people deal with the fact they are dying and help them and their families face it. In our case, we began telling them that we knew Jeff was dying, had probably only a few weeks to live, and that while we weren't happy about it, we also had a strong faith that was sustaining us both. We chatted for over an hour and when they left, they thanked US for ministering to THEM.

I remembered what my choir had told me about his last Sunday in church, just five days before he died. He had been insistent that I find someone to come pick him up and get him to Zion. I had to leave too early to be able to take him. So I called a couple and asked the favor, no small one since we lived a 45-minute drive from the church. They brought him in a wheelchair. From the organ bench where I sat, I couldn't see him but many in my choir could. They told me how he paid rapt attention to the entire service, participating as much as he could. When it was time for communion, instead of waiting for the ministers to bring it to him, which would normally be done for anyone in a wheelchair, he began to wheel the chair forward. He was so eager to receive the sacrament. His modeling of what it means to be a Christian at such a time was a tremendous witness. Many have told me how moved they were by his presence.

Our priest, Fr. Miller, has commented that he showed us how to die. Indeed, he did. So now my memories are a great blessing to me. I thank God for the fantastic three plus decades we had together. I'm so grateful for all that we shared. God is so good. Now I face the challenge of learning to live a life without Jeff that will bring God glory with whatever time I have. Given the longevity in my family tree that could be a very long time indeed. If I live to my mother's age, I will be a widow for 40 years!

Widow

Jeff has finished his life on this earth and gone to be with his Lord. But for me, life as a widow is just beginning. Until recently I had never given much thought to what that would be like. Now I stare into the future and wonder if I can cope. Yes, I can balance the checkbook; I've always been the one to do that. I can mow the lawn; that's something I usually did too. But can I stand the loneliness of coming home to an empty house? How will I take vacations? Where will I go and what will I do? Will I have enough money to do anything? Although these questions are pushed to the background as you deal with the immediacy of a funeral, they are never far away.

There are endless forms to fill out during the first weeks. I remember well the first few times I had to check the box marked "widow" on these forms. But what really sent me into an emotional spiral was the first time I had a choice between "married" and "single" and realized with a lump in my throat that I had to check "single". For 31 years I had been "married" and sometimes I would even playfully add "very happily" to the "married" box. Now it seemed like someone had hit me in the stomach as I tearfully checked the "single" box.

I know that I am single now, but I still feel like I'm married. So far I have continued to wear my wedding ring. It seems right for me. Jeff and I were too close for too long to be able to just change gears in my thinking. The day may come when I'll remove the ring, but for now it stays put.

Nevertheless, I am a widow. I cannot shrink from that fact. And I have actually found it helpful to use the word in referring to myself when it is appropriate. It helps to make it more real for me and therefore I'm better able to accept the reality. So as I introduce myself to my new neighbors, for instance, I will explain that I live by myself because I am a widow. This could be taken as a play for sympathy, but for me it is simply stating a fact that I now have to live with.

Holidays and Anniversaries

When I became a widow, I was well acquainted with the idea that birthdays and holidays were supposed to be difficult times. Since we had celebrated both our birthdays, as well as Christmas and our anniversary, in the last several months prior to my husband's death, I was given a long time before I had to face any of those things. However, the day came when I realized that Thanksgiving and my birthday (which, in that first year, coincided) would be coming up and I had no plans. In fact, this began to bother me back in September, three months before the date. I would be sitting at the organ practicing and my mind would wander to Thanksgiving and the fact that I had no place to go. I would dissolve in a puddle of tears, thankful that no one was around to know. What do you do when your only child lives 2,000 miles away and no other relatives that would think to invite you live any closer? Since I play for the Thanksgiving service at 10 a.m., I'm not free to go very far away anyhow.

Fr. Miller and his wife told me that I would always be welcome at their home on holidays and I know they mean it. But I wasn't sure I had the nerve to ask even so. And then I found out that they were going out of town this year. That sent me into another tailspin. Good friends on Long Island apologized for not being able to squeeze me in with their family gathering but we both agreed the drive was too long since I couldn't leave before 11 a.m. anyway. So, one by one, possibilities seemed to evaporate.

I even toyed with the idea that maybe I should stop feeling so sorry for myself and invite others in similar shoes to come to *my* house. But the only ones I could think of had family in the area or were traveling to be with children. And I really didn't want to do that anyway. So I was back to having a pity party and not knowing what to do. Early in November Fr. Miller asked casually one time what my plans were for the holiday. I replied that I didn't know and beat a hasty retreat lest my tears become too obvious.

That's when I finally came to my senses and realized I needed help. So a few days later I knocked on Fr. Miller's office door. I explained that I had no place to go and that it had become a really charged emotional issue for me. He asked if I would allow him to help. Of course, I would! That's why I was there. He explained that he would arrange for a family to invite me. He had done this before for others and was happy to be of help. It was a great relief to have finally admitted to someone how upset I was.

Several days later I received a call from a family in the parish inviting me for Thanksgiving. I don't know how much they had been told and it didn't matter. The important thing for me was that I now had a place to go for the holiday and wonderful people to be with. What a blessing that day was for me. I enjoyed it immensely.

The next big hurdle was our anniversary six days before Christmas. At that time of year, I am so busy as a church musician that it was fairly easy not to get too bogged down. My very good friends, Fr. Jim and Chris, wanted me to come for Christmas. My son and his wife would be arriving the day after, so the timing was perfect. I played the Christmas Eve services, got up early on Christmas Day and drove to Long Island ahead of a major snowstorm. I spent a wonderful day with my friends and stayed the night. By the next day, the roads were being cleared from the eight or nine inches of snow and I was able to get back to Poughkeepsie a few hours ahead of my son's arrival.

On Jeff's birthday I went to Mass and remembered him there. (His ashes are in the wall of the columbarium garden just outside the chapel where the weekday Masses are held.) I remembered back to the previous year when Jeff had made one last effort and said Mass for the Sisters at the Convent. (Before his illness, part of his job was to say Mass for them six days a week.) It was the last time he felt well enough to celebrate the Eucharist and it had been on his birthday. I'm so grateful that I was there that day.

The anniversary of his death is harder to pin down. I know the date: March 22. But the year he died, that was 2 days before Holy Week began. So in many ways that is more of an anniversary to me that the actual date. I ended up remembering both times but without undue stress.

For me, the hardest times seem to be the holidays that are so closely linked with family. Not only do I no longer have a spouse, but what family I have outside my son is not close enough (in terms of bonding) to be of any help. And at this point in my son's career (a Captain in the Air Force, who is currently teaching pilots to fly jets), he is too far away physically. That may change at some point in the future but for now it's the reality we both live with. When people commiserate with me about Matt being so far away, I point out that compared with the previous 4 years when he was in Korea and Japan, it seems like he is just around the corner. And we can talk anytime we like without having to deal with a 12- or 13-hour time difference and international phone rates. So I'm very grateful.

Going Out

One of the things that I know about myself is that I am basically shy and I'm an introvert. That means it isn't easy to make casual friends. Jeff has always been my best friend and the person with whom I always did things. If we were in a social situation, he knew how to make small talk and I stuck with him. And for the last two years since we moved, I've had little opportunity to make friends. My church is a 45-minute drive away so there was little chance to socialize with the people there. Living on the grounds of a Convent didn't do much for a social life either. We joined a local community chorus. We both love to sing and have always found a group to join everywhere we have lived. But that isn't a very good way to get to know people since we spend all our time singing, not socializing.

I knew that I would have to push myself to get out and get to know people. So I made it a rule that, at least for the first year, anytime some asked me to do something or go somewhere, I would automatically say "yes," even if it was something I wouldn't ordinarily do.

That almost got me into trouble once. "Would you like to go see the new James Bond flick?" my choir member asked. He had been a tremendous help to me just after I moved into my house in Poughkeepsie. There were numerous tasks that required a second set of hands and often some handyman expertise that I didn't have. So he had willingly come to my house several times and helped. I knew he had a "lady friend." So when he asked I immediately said yes. Then I got to thinking that he might consider this a date. So when he called later to make the arrangements I decided to be totally upfront. I told him that if this was two friends going to the movies (Dutch treat), then I would be happy to go. But if he considered this a date, I wasn't interested. He appreciated my honesty and assured me it was two friends going to a movie together. With that understanding I felt free to go.

I'm not used to thinking about such things or about appearances. But I know that now I need to. I don't want to give a wrong impression to anyone. So I will continue to be up front about what I'm thinking and let the chips fall where they may.

I do know that Jeff wanted me to feel free to remarry. His own father had remarried several years after the death of his mother. And while that caused a few tensions in the families, we all acknowledged that it was wonderful for the two of them. We had told each other occasionally over the years that we each wanted this for the other should something happen. But he repeated it to me at a time when it was anything but theoretical.

Ten months before his cancer diagnosis he went to his G.P. on a Monday after feeling lousy all weekend. He thought he might have the flu. The doctor had a different opinion. He sent him straight to the surgeon who palpated his abdomen and sent him directly to the hospital (do not pass go, do not collect $200). He ordered an X-ray, CT scan, and several other tests and said he would meet us in the emergency room. When he arrived, Jeff had only had the X-ray, but that was enough for the surgeon. He could see something leaking into the abdominal cavity. He told us immediate surgery was necessary. He didn't know what the problem was, but it could be serious, even life threatening.

He would have to deal with whatever he found once he opened him up.

When the surgeon left to prep, Jeff handed me his Palm Pilot and cell phone and told me to call a few key people to get some prayers started. I had to step outside the hospital to use the cell phone. When I came back Jeff was alone, waiting on the gurney to be wheeled into surgery. He took my hand, looked me in the eye and said, "I just want you to know that if anything happens to me I want you to feel free to remarry." On one level, I appreciated his saying it, but that wasn't what I wanted to talk about just then. So I acknowledged his comment and quickly changed the subject.

The surgery revealed a perforated colon which was repaired by removing part of it and giving him a temporary colostomy. So we thought we had a permanent reprieve from thinking about death. It's a real blessing that we can't see into the future.

Shrine Mont 2002

Region 2 of the Order of St. Luke, the ecumenical healing order in the church, holds its annual spring conference at a retreat facility in Orkney Springs, Virginia called Shrine Mont. Jeff was scheduled to be the keynote speaker in 2002. He died two months before that. I had planned on going with him. Now what do I do? Many of my friends from Long Island will be there including my close friends, Fr. Jim and Chris. It's been 2 years since we moved off the Island and I miss not having time with them. But could I really handle a conference on healing where Jeff was to have been the speaker? I hesitate. It's a tough call. But finally, my desire to spend time with some longtime friends wins out.

Chris is in charge of the music ministry and I sing with them and play the piano when I'm there. So I can't hide in the background. And I find it very painful to hear another speaker knowing how much Jeff had been looking forward to that opportunity. Why couldn't he have been healed. So many, many people are. I still believe very much in the healing ministry, but it surely is a mystery.

We sang *Lift High the Cross* at the opening service and Fr. Jim reminded me that we had sung that at Jeff's funeral. I had momentarily forgotten. Once he took me back to that memory, I had a hard time playing it. When your eyes are wet with tears the notes on the page look more like a Rorschach test than a piece of music.

It was indeed great to be with my friends from Long Island, but the next day during a break I was nevertheless feeling very alone. I went back to my room and before long I was crying. Then I was sobbing. Chris came into the cabin where we were all staying and heard me. She knocked on my door, came in, and put her arm around me. She let me cry for a while and when I had calmed down a bit we talked. I wanted to take a walk and she agreed to go with me. I've never been so thankful for a true friend. She didn't try to talk me out of what I was feeling. She was simply there for me.

Fr. Jim was equally helpful, letting me cry on his shoulder and blubber about how miserable I was. It was a good release for me. I couldn't have let down my guard that much with most of my new friends. I just don't know them that well yet. Here were two people with whom I could be totally myself. What a gift! I hope I can be there that way for someone sometime.

Shrine Mont 2003

This year I know that I will attend the Shrine Mont Conference. I've agreed to give a workshop on the place of music in worship and the healing ministry. Three weeks before, I get a phone call early in the morning. "Beverly, this is Claire. I wanted you to know before you get the general e-mail that Fr. Jim died last night." What? How could that be? He wasn't even sick.

He was on his way home from a Bible Study when he had a massive heart attack and died instantly. I was shocked. What should I do? Should I call Chris. She had probably been up all night and didn't need to be bothered so early. Besides, she would have so much to attend to, decisions to make, people to notify. By the time I got to work, I knew I had to call, even if I didn't reach her.

She answered on the first ring. Yes, she was devastated and probably in a state of shock. But she obviously appreciated hearing from me. We talked about some of the arrangements she would have to make and she seemed able to think clearly about the things that needed doing. Two of her children were with her and the third was flying in later that day. So at least she would have family there. I promised to come for the funeral. I let her know that I would be praying for her. The rest of that day, as I went about my job in a state of shock, she was never far from my thoughts. And true to my word, I prayed for her constantly.

During the next two days, I was continually thinking of things I wanted to tell her and share with her. At first, I thought I would tell her at the funeral. Then I realized I wouldn't really have time to talk with her: there would be too many people there. (It was held in the Cathedral in Garden City with a luncheon in her parish church in Setauket following.) So then I decided to put some thoughts on paper. I ended up writing a two-page letter on the computer, which I then gave her at the luncheon. I told her to read it later when she had time. She has since told me that she has referred to it on several occasions and found it very helpful. I'm glad.

Chris now faced an even harder decision than I'd had the previous year. Fr. Jim was to have been the coordinator of the Shrine Mont conference and she was to lead the music team. Should she go? It was less than 3 weeks away. I didn't try to tell her what to do but I did offer to room with her *if* she decided to go. She was most grateful and that's exactly what happened. So here we were exactly a year after she and Fr. Jim had been such a help to me. Now Jeff was showing Fr. Jim around the heavenly realm and I was left to help pick up the pieces with Chris. When I asked God to use me someday to help someone else, I certainly hadn't wanted or expected it to be one of my very best friends and only a year later!

Why Me?

Today would have been our 32nd wedding anniversary. When I
said Morning Prayer, I began to wonder why Jeff, who was
such a good preacher, couldn't have lived longer. With his
incredible ability to preach and touch people's lives, why am I
the one left?

He was in his prime as a teacher and preacher. Most people
who heard his sermons found them insightful and helpful.
They never noticed that they tended to be longer than is
average in our denomination. He was that good a speaker.

Perhaps his greatest love was in being able to help people on
their spiritual journey through what is often called Spiritual
Direction. Both clergy and lay people came to him with
questions and problems or just routine boredom and he
listened, prayed, and often gave advice. He had a way of
understanding the problem behind the problem and cutting to
the core of the issue. He loved helping them develop a prayer
life and teaching them how to get closer to God.

So as I sat praying and remembering all that he had hoped to
accomplish in the next 20 or so years, I was filled with sadness.
Before long I was crying big tears. "Why did Jeff have to be the
one to die? He had so much more to offer the Lord than I do.
He was such a good preacher." I just couldn't get over the
feeling that it wasn't right.

At Bible study later that morning, my friend Virginia was
making a point about something in the lesson. She turned to me

and said, "It's just like the way you preach through your music. It is so powerful." I was startled at her use of the word "preach." I had never had anyone apply that to my music ministry before. I immediately associated her comment with my prayer earlier in the morning about Jeff being such a good preacher. She went on for a few more sentences and then stopped. She got a funny look on her face. Then she said that she really didn't know why she had used the word "preach" in connection with my music. It had never occurred to her to use it in that context. But I knew. God was telling me (through her) that Jeff wasn't the only preacher in the family. It was His way of affirming that my ministry may be different, but I should never look on it as inferior to the one Jeff had. Amazing! I admit I have trouble believing it but I'm working on it.

The Presence of God

An experience of the presence of God is always an awesome one. It never happens when you expect it and certainly not when you think you need it most. At least, that has been my experience.

When Jeff had his emergency surgery, he encountered Jesus in a powerful way. As he lay on the gurney waiting, while I was outside calling friends to start praying, he swears that Jesus walked through the curtain into the cubicle where he was. It was not a vision or a physical manifestation, just the sure and certain knowledge that He was there. It was so powerful that it took away all fear and even left him ambivalent about whether he lived or died. The feeling stayed with him the entire week in the hospital. When he spoke of it months later at a healing conference, he was radiant.

At that point, I had experienced a number of times when God had seemed close but nothing of that magnitude.

After Jeff's cancer surgery when he was recuperating at home, he had a similar epiphany. He had been out on our deck all morning. It was a bright sunny day in the early fall and I figured he was doing some reading and praying. About noon I joined him for a chat and to see if he was ready for lunch. He began to tell me that he had spent the whole morning in prayer. It was another time when for him God was RIGHT THERE. He felt enveloped in the love of God. Then he turned to me with an almost apologetic look on his face as he said, "God was *so* close this morning. And I know He loves me so very much. I could have asked Him for anything. But I didn't want to, not even to be healed. God knows I want to be healed and He loves me so much He will do what is best."

I was momentarily stunned when he said he couldn't ask to be healed. But then I understood, at least partly. God is Goodness personified. He loves Jeff far more even than I do. We had prayed many times that God would heal Jeff and He certainly knows that is what *we* want. But He knows the bigger picture that we can't even guess. And because we trust that love I can understand, at least with my head, why Jeff felt that way.

That doesn't for a moment mean that we didn't have a very rough road ahead. We certainly walked through the valley of the shadow of death together. We experienced all the emotions from anger to despair to depression. But we were also able, before his death, to come to some acceptance. And through it all, even when we didn't "feel" it, we knew on some level that God was with us and that He loved us more than we could possibly imagine.

My own extremely powerful experience of God's presence and love came almost a year after Jeff's death. I was sitting in the living room of the home of my spiritual director. We were talking about my prayer life and she was responding to something I had said. All of a sudden, I realized that the presence of God was filling that room, or at least me. The love of God was washing over me in waves. I struggled to concentrate on what was being said and then gave up. I slumped back in my chair and did the only thing I could do: I closed my eyes and gave myself over to the experience. I was so overcome I don't think I could have gotten out of the chair if the house had been on fire. And now I understand in a whole new way how, when God comes that close, you have no desire to ask for anything. God is so loving that there is no need to ask for anything. None of us are exempt from pain and suffering. That's part of what it means to be human. But experiencing that divine love makes it easier to trust that no matter what it looks like to us, God really does have it all under control. He will see us through no matter what!

The Revolt of the Inanimate Objects

I grew up assuming that all men were handy around the house. There was nothing my father couldn't fix. He had a basement full of old fans, record players, and junk of every variety, along with tools galore. Although I don't remember my grandfather in any great detail, I do remember that his basement was also full of tools. My brother certainly inherited that ability to do necessary home repairs. So when I married Jeff I just assumed that he would be like them. I was not disappointed. His father was an electric engineer so when we wanted a dimmer on the dining room light, he did it. If the snow blower wasn't working properly: take it apart and see if you can figure it out.

When my son was with me for the funeral, I asked him to take a look at the lawnmower and make sure it would start. The time for grass cutting was just around the corner. He started it up and assured me everything was set. And it was the first time I used it. The second time, however, it refused to start. I couldn't pull the cord. The advantage of still living at the Convent at that point was that I could go find the maintenance man and ask for help. He declared it unfixable. It would have to go to the repair shop. I couldn't even lift it into the trunk of the car without help. I didn't need this so early in my widowhood. Tears flowed. Then I pulled myself together and took it in for repair. Little did I know this was just the beginning of the revolt of inanimate objects.

When I bought my house, I wanted to take my much newer dishwasher from the house at the Convent. A friend uninstalled it easily and I was looking forward to the same at my new home. However, after an hour of trying everything, my friends couldn't budge the old one. Then we discovered that the relatively new kitchen floor had been put in when the dishwasher was in place. They had added a new sub floor which now meant the dishwasher couldn't slide out. A large plumbing bill later and I finally had my dishwasher.

My cell phone turned into another headache. The one my husband had used wouldn't work in my new location. So I got another one that was advertised to work anywhere cell service was available. I believed it and bought the phone. Since I only used it for emergencies it was more than a month before I found out that it wouldn't work anywhere south of where I lived. That meant that I had no coverage during my weekly trips to Westchester County or my monthly visits to Long Island. And with an old car, those were exactly the places I most wanted to know I was covered in an emergency. After numerous phone calls that got me nowhere, I reported the company to the Consumer Protection Board and after another several months finally got a refund. The simplest things can become such big projects.

The all-time biggest frustration came with the computer. I moved into my new home, got everything set up and couldn't manage to get online. After several weeks and help from a number of friends, it was discovered that the problem wasn't my computer at all. The phone line into the house was not working properly for the computer. I called the phone company and the man who came tweaked something outside and it started working. My relief was short lived. Within a few days I was back to having major trouble. This call to the phone company did not produce the desired results. The operator informed me that the phone line was guaranteed for voice, not data. It was my problem, there would be no further help from them. An older man in my parish, when he heard about it, pronounced that as rubbish. He volunteered to help me call the phone company and talk to them in a way they would understand. Since he used to troubleshoot computers for IBM and had had a similar problem in his own home, I knew he was the one to help. We agreed to wait until after the Christmas holiday which was fast approaching.

In the meantime, I noticed lots of phone company trucks doing a lot of work about 3 or 4 blocks from my house. This went on for over a week. I have no idea what they were doing. But at the end of it, my computer had no trouble getting on line and has worked fine ever since.

Lest I get too complacent, it was time for another mechanical breakdown. We were having one of the snowiest winters in recent memory, so my snowblower was a real Godsend. When I returned to Poughkeepsie the day after Christmas, just a few hours ahead of my son's arrival, I anticipated using the blower to remove the eight or nine inches of snow from the driveway that had fallen the day before. It was very sluggish as I started it up and pretty soon it gave up the ghost. I did a little by hand and left the rest for Matt and Cathy. This time I had to be sympathetic with the snow blower. It was 14 years old and had never had any maintenance. So when I took it in to the shop I had to admit it was overdue.

As a homeowner, I know that there will always be problems. I was hoping to be spared most of them for a little while. But it seemed like that first year, all the things that could go wrong, did. I was on a fast learning curve of what to do to get things fixed and where to take them.

Father Gadget

Jeff was one of the original "techies." As a physics major in college he had taken a computer course back in the 60's. So when PCs were just coming on the market, he invested in one. It seemed that we upgraded every year until we finally reached the stage of laptops that would keep him happy for several years at a time. (Then, when he did upgrade, I would get the cast off.)

But anything dealing with technology fascinated him. Again, before they were popular, he had a GPS (global positioning system), which he mounted in the car to help him find where he was going. We also used it on some of our travels. In Nepal, he was holding it out the window of a taxi one time to try to get better reception. The driver got spooked by this "thing" and needed reassurance from our interpreter that it wasn't some kind of weapon.

The first Palm Pilot quickly replaced the pocket calendar for all of his appointments. In fact, it was so well known around the parish that he couldn't do anything without it that people would ask if he had his "brain" with him. They knew no business could be conducted unless his Palm was in his hand.

His secretary finally had enough and one day called him "Father Gadget." The name stuck and became a parish joke.

All of this presented me with a problem after his death. I am a far cry from a "techie" and needed to either learn how to use some of the gadgets or get rid of them. I quickly decided to get rid of the GPS and several smaller computer related gadgets. I kept the Palm and just used it for addresses and phone numbers until the screen cracked after a year. Then I threw it out and got a small pocket organizer that was more what I could use.

The computer has been a bigger challenge. He had told me that I should begin using his newer and better computer after he died. I decided that I should tackle that immediately. With my son's help in deleting a number of unnecessary programs, I have made some progress in learning how to work it. I already knew the basics of Word and e-mail. I also use the database program that he created for me in Access. I have over 4,000 entries in my organ music and over 1,000 for the choral library at church. I try to keep it backed up with the old computer at church and this good one. But if anything ever goes wrong I don't know what I'll do. I try not to think about it. Whenever I have a problem with it, I can't help thinking, "If only Jeff were here. He'd know what to do."

I Must Be Sure to Tell Jeff…

Some people I've spoken with have had experiences of a deceased loved one appearing to them in a dream or vision or when they were praying. I'm sure such an experience would be comforting. But that has not been the case with me nor did I expect it to be. I only came close on one occasion.

A week after Jeff's funeral there was a mission being held by the Order of St. Luke, an ecumenical group that believes in prayer for healing. Jeff and I were involved in the healing ministry for over 15 years, but only after moving to Peekskill did we actually join the Order of St. Luke. Since I wanted to get in the habit of going out when I had an opportunity, I decided to attend. There was a small group and the speaker, Nigel Mumford, was a friend of ours. (He had read a lesson and been a pallbearer at Jeff's funeral.) At the end of the day there was a time for praying with people and Nigel asked if it would be ok for the whole group to pray with me before they went on to individual prayer.

I am always eager to be prayed with so of course I said yes. I sat in a chair in the center of the room and Nigel stood in front of me praying while the others gathered around and laid hands on me. Nigel had previously told me how he had felt Jeff standing beside him the night before when he was speaking. So perhaps that was in my mind as they started to pray. For a moment or two I thought I could sense Jeff standing with Nigel with a really big grin on his face. It was a fleeting thought and it reduced me to tears, but it was also typically Jeff. So whatever was really going on, I like to think of Jeff with that big silly smile. I know he has been interceding for me ever since his departure and I'm sure that is one of the reasons I've managed as well as I have.

But even after more than a year I will often be somewhere and something will happen that I'll want to share. It is still instinctive to think, "I must be sure to tell Jeff …" And then I realize that I can't, of course. But I also know that if it is anything he needs to know, he already does!

Doctors

Many of us, I believe, rely on our spouses to give us the occasional prod to get to the doctor. We certainly did that for each other. I'm not sure when Jeff would have ever made a dentist appointment if I hadn't insisted. And when I had a pain that just wouldn't go away, he would keep after me until I agreed to see the doctor.

Jeff had ulcerative colitis for almost 30 years, which meant having a colonoscopy every year or two. I was always glad that I didn't have to have such a test. However, the year of Jeff's cancer diagnosis, but several months prior, my gynecologist strongly urged me to have one. I was well over 50 and it was time, she said. Jeff encouraged me to follow through, so I made an appointment for a month after his surgery. Imagine my shock and surprise when the doctor informed me that he had removed two polyps and that one was cancerous (not just "pre-cancerous"). He was as dumbfounded as I. He was all too aware of the irony of the situation with my husband having been diagnosed the month before with colon cancer. And in fact, he had done the colonoscopy on Jeff four months before the surgery that had shown nothing suspicious.

Well, this was more than suspicious. He sent me for tests and had three different labs look at the polyp. All agreed that it was totally encapsulated and no further treatment was needed. Whew! Jeff told me later that his first reaction on hearing the news was, "Coffin for two, please." I was still trying to cope with Jeff's diagnosis and didn't need one of my own. Praise God everything was ok after all.

Now, however, I have to police myself and make sure I don't forget that yearly colonoscopy. And having moved six months ago, I have to convince new doctors that it is important. Trying to schedule one has been frustrating. My GP insists that he will notify the office of the doctor that he wants me to see and *they* will call *me*. That step takes five days. Then I'm informed that I have to have a telephone consultation with the doctor before a time can be set for the procedure. So we agree on a time for that. Then she calls back and has to change it. The day of the phone call, I wait by the phone for an hour before and an hour after the appointed time but no call comes.

The next day, I call the scheduler who says she will notify the office and get back to me. 36 hours later, having heard nothing, I call again. By now I am getting frustrated and explain that this is not just routine: I did have cancer and I don't want to fall in the scheduling crack. In desperation, she gives me the number of the office to call where they actually schedule the procedure. Finally, I find myself talking to the person who can straighten this out. And she does. Within 5 minutes she has scheduled me for the phone consultation *and* the procedure, a month ahead of when I was actually looking to have it. She seems to think that given my history, why wait?

I find all of this very draining. And much of it has to do with moving and finding all new physicians. At least after this first round of doctors' appointments I will know who I am dealing with. It will be an enormous relief when I have finally met all the regular ones and they have my history. I can better understand now why older people hate to move. It isn't just the move itself and the leaving of friends, it is the hassle of starting over with doctors who don't know you and understand your particular set of problems. It takes a lot of energy to be forceful in making sure they understand what your needs are. You really do have to take charge of your own health care or don't be surprised if you fall in the crack. You owe it to yourself and your children to take good care of yourself.

Vacations

As a priest, Jeff was entitled to a month of vacation each year and we always took the allotted time to get away. Dealing with people and their joys and sorrows can take an emotional toll, and we looked forward to that month each summer. Our ideal vacation was a camping trip to the Adirondack's and a canoe trip in Algonquin Park, Ontario. Those weren't always our destinations: we camped all over the United States. But those were the two places we kept going back to.

During the dull days of winter, I would pull out the maps of Algonquin Park and start planning possible canoe routes. Jeff always wanted to know how many portages there were (since he had to portage the canoe) before he would agree to an itinerary. After that was settled and confirmed by the Park authorities, I would begin to plan the menus.

Our canoe trips were usually 10–14 days in length, so planning meals was an exact science. After the first day or two, it was all freeze dried or packaged food. (No bottles or cans are allowed.) I had to consider size and weight and make sure it would all fit in one large pack.

Another pack carried our clothes for two weeks and the final two packs held our tent, sleeping pads and sleeping bags, cooking pots and utensils, etc. By the time we were ready to leave in the summer, I knew which pocket of which pack held each item. And I loved the planning part almost as much as the trip itself.

But now what do I do? Does a 57-year-old widow go camping and canoeing by herself? I don't think so. At least, not this first summer. One of the first things I did after Jeff's death was to sell our truck and camper. It made no sense to keep it. I still have the canoes (a tandem that was ours and a solo that is our son's) and all the packs, tents, etc. So if I ever want to try it again I can. But for now, I need another plan.

We had heard of Elderhostel from some friends and Jeff suggested that I check that out for a possible way to vacation. After his death, I did just that. I knew I needed to plan something to really look forward to. Summer would be hard without our usual camping trip. So as I looked through their catalogs of possibilities (which seemed endless), I was struck with a trip to explore Wales. I don't know why that particular one attracted me, but I thought about it for a week or so and mentioned it to a few friends. Then I called and signed up! Now I had something to anticipate in August. That was important to me.

I enjoyed the trip and am going on an Elderhostel in Canada this year. It is in a Forest Preserve near Algonquin Park where we used to canoe. It will get me outdoors, which I miss when I don't have that opportunity. In fact, I decided that this year I would even try a bit of solo camping in the Adirondacks. (Solo canoe camping would be too hard and too dangerous, so that is out.) I can take our son's solo canoe for day trips and I'll stay in our favorite campground, Fish Creek, at night. There will be other people in the campground and the waters where I'll canoe will have other boaters as well. So if I get into trouble help will be close at hand.

The jury is still out. I may find that I love it, even on my own, and will do it again in the future. Or I may find that I needed to do this for closure. In that case I will no doubt continue to find other ways to spend time in God's wonderful creation.

Salary Cut – Now What?

"The Vestry has had to make some hard decisions in order to rein in the budget for next year. It will no longer be possible to fund the Sunday evening service."

We were gathered in Fr. Miller's office in the middle of June. The announced budget cut would impact me substantially. When the service began nine months ago it was, for me, a remarkable answer to prayer. In the months following Jeff's death, as I put together a budget, it became obvious that I would have a gap between income and expenses. But just about that time I was told about the Sunday evening service. The amount of extra income it would generate for me was almost exactly the amount of my budget short fall. Wow! God is so good.

I also knew that this was an experiment and that it was only guaranteed for a year. Now I'm being told that it will last until the end of the current year, which is actually a total of 16 months. And, I'm being given six months of lead time to figure out what to do. I'm very grateful for that!

Nevertheless, my immediate emotional reaction is not only disappointment (I loved the alternative service where I played the piano instead of the organ and we sang a different style of music), but a mild degree of panic. I thought God had taken care of my problem and now it's being thrown back in my lap. How will I cope?

After buying my house I don't have a lot of assets left. With the market in such bad shape, I don't think they will generate enough income to close the gap. And I will *not* take down the remaining principle.

An obvious solution might be to start teaching piano. I have resisted that up until now. I've enjoyed the freedom of not being tied down to a tight schedule. I taught when my son was very little. When he started school, I realized that if I continued to teach it would negate the whole reason I was a stay-at-home mom. When he walked in the door from school so did my first piano student. So instead of being available for Matt, I was telling him to go play and get out of my hair so I could teach. When I realized what was happening, I stopped teaching to be available for my son.

My husband and I had agreed from the beginning that we would live on his income. Whatever income I brought in from a church job or teaching would be the gravy. It enabled us to do things we couldn't have otherwise, and it paid for our vacations. Even when my son grew up and left home and I continued to work in the church (more demanding positions), it was always part-time. A priest works such long and often unpredictable hours that I wanted to be there to do as much as I could around the house (yes, mowing the lawn and often taking out the garbage) so when he did have time off, we could enjoy it together. A full-time job would not have been compatible with his day off on Monday, either. So we were both very happy with my part time jobs.

But now I have a half-time job at the church, a pension from my husband, and a considerable budget gap. After getting the news, I went back to the church to practice. Before sitting down at the organ, I knelt at the altar and put it all in God's hands. I asked Him to show me what to do. Unfortunately, that doesn't mean I stopped worrying. But as I went through the evening, I kept turning it back over to God. At one point I decided to sit down at the piano and sing some praise songs. The first one was "Jehovah Jireh, My Provider." Yes, I believe that God will provide the answer. I went on and found myself singing a song of dedication, offering God my life and everything I have been through to be used for His glory. I had no trouble meaning that one. Next my eye fell on a favorite of mine, "God Will Make a Way Where There Seems to Be No Way." I cried my way through these songs. God is faithful and He *will* show me the way. Ok! Everything will be all right. I'm beginning to get the picture. TRUST GOD.

I was rather surprised to find that when I woke up in the night instead of worrying or even thinking of my situation, I was generating ideas for this book. I even grabbed pencil and paper to jot down a few thoughts.

The next day I went to a workshop sponsored by the American Guild of Organists. One of my colleagues, Susan, began telling me about her piano teaching. We chatted and I realized that if I am to start teaching again, I need some pointers on methods, etc. So we have agreed to get together this week. Her church job is very similar to mine and yet she has 30 students! I was flabbergasted. I was thinking that if I can get 13 students, I can break even with what I was making on the Sunday night service. If she can do twice as many, plus be a wife and mother, then surely I could manage.

It was now Saturday afternoon and I had been wanting to attend a small local parish where a good friend is the priest. They have their liturgy on Saturday at 5:00 p.m. I was looking forward to seeing how she does things, but more importantly, it would be a chance for me to worship with *no* other responsibilities. This seemed like a good day to go. The minute I walked in and sat down, I sensed that God was waiting for me. Before the service started, I was caught up in the joy of being able to worship my creator and redeemer. It wasn't a bubbly joy but a profoundly deep experience of God's love and care.

The liturgy was nothing extraordinary. It was about 20 people gathered together as family to worship. The old reed organ wheezed through the hymns. The words were the familiar ones from the Book of Common Prayer. But for me it was a very holy time. I was able to enter into worship in a way that I usually can't when I am busy with the mechanics of being the organist and choir director. And even though I attend weekday Masses where I don't have those responsibilities, they are without music. And for me, music is a very big entry point for the Holy Spirit. Singing even a simple Taizé chant can open me up to the Godhead like nothing else can.

By the end of the service I realized something rather remarkable. I was thinking about teaching piano in the fall and not only feeling positive about it but looking forward to it. It was no longer just something I would have to do. In leaving, I was chatting with the organist who asked if I had any organ students. I explained that I didn't have *any* students yet but that I would be looking for some in the fall. She indicated that she might like to come for a few organ lessons. Well, God. Your ways may not be my ways, but how could I ever doubt your Goodness!

In All Circumstances, Give Thanks

When my life was going well and I had only minor complaints, this verse from I Thessalonians 5:18 seemed easy enough. We are reminded to always be joyful, to pray continually, and to give thanks in all circumstances because this is God's will for us in Christ Jesus. Now I look and say, "How is that possible?"

The problem, I think, centers around a preposition. We read this verse and assume that we are somehow supposed to ignore our pain and anger and other emotions and give thanks for everything that happens to us. What we fail to realize, at least I failed to recognize, is that we are not expected to thank God for all the bad things that happen to us. Rather, in the midst of conditions that we can't control and may not be at all to our liking, we can still thank God. We are not thanking him FOR those situations, but IN SPITE OF them.

No matter how bad life seems to be at the moment, we can always find reasons to thank God. I had to let God remind me of that very recently. I was feeling down for a number of compelling reasons: I'm experiencing numbness in my arm, hand, and leg, which, for a musician, could spell disaster; my salary will be substantially reduced at the end of the year when my duties change; I was facing a colonoscopy; hot flashes have been a real annoyance ever since I went off hormone replacement therapy four months ago, etc. You get the picture. I was having a good old-fashioned pity party. How dare God ask me to give thanks!

That's when I took another look at the preposition. God wasn't asking me to give thanks FOR these circumstances. But in the midst of all this, He was still expecting me to be able to give thanks. And I realized I could. I thanked Him for the roof over my head and the food on my table. I praised Him for friends and family. I thanked Him for the privilege of living in a country where I can worship Him anytime and anywhere I want. I am grateful for a wonderful spiritual director and for a Rector who is a joy to work for and with. I greatly appreciate a son and daughter-in-law who make every effort to stay in touch and are concerned for my wellbeing.

As I began to give thanks, my mood also began to change. It was almost imperceptible at first. After all, I felt entitled to my misery. But then I had to make a decision. Did I really want to stay dejected or was I willing to let God show me how much I really had to be thankful for? It has been a case of two steps forward and one step backward some of the time. But the overall movement is definitely in a positive direction.

Yes, it is possible to give thanks to God IN all circumstances.

Loneliness

Anyone who has lost a spouse through death would agree that it is a very lonely existence for the remaining person. Many married couples, myself included, would tell you that being married is like being one half of a whole. People joke about "my better half" or "my other half." But for the truly married, this is reality. When that bond is severed, whether quickly or long anticipated, the remaining person feels a lot like an inch worm that has been cut in half. We wait in vain for the other half to grow back. Finally, we realize we are truly alone and it HURTS.

I always looked forward to the dinner hour when Jeff and I would share all the little things that had happened during the day: my frustration at having to wait so long in the doctor's office, Jeff's joy at helping a parishioner who is seeking a deeper prayer life, my delight at having finally gotten a passage in a Bach fugue to sound right, his disappointment in a sermon that wasn't coming together yet. We shared it all.

Now, other than talking to the cats (which I do on occasion), there is no one to share with. So I have made a decision of the will. I want to use this opportunity (that I didn't ask for but is nevertheless there) to get closer to God. I certainly have more time and I want to put it to good use. So I told God and my spiritual director that I want to "work" on my spiritual life.

Does that keep me from experiencing loneliness? Of course not. But it does give me an outlet. I can and do turn to God much more frequently and share with Him all my feelings and concerns. And I know that even though I can't feel it most of the time, this time of bereavement can be a time of growth in the Spirit if I let it. And so I pray for an intensification of my life with God. I want to be open to all that He has for me; to learn to recognize His hand in my life and follow where He leads.

It is not a cure for loneliness. There are times when I need God to have human arms to hug me and a shoulder to cry on. I'm not as strong as others think I am and as I sometimes like to think I am. But loneliness can be an avenue to the Divine if we want it to be. The God who made me and Jeff and brought us together in the first place is the God who can now teach me the next step in my life with Him.

Cats

I believe I was born loving animals. I am fascinated by wild animals and have always been thrilled when, on our camping trips, we have come across bears, moose, skunks, and even chipmunks and marmots. But most of all, I love cats. Dogs are great, too, but my real affection is reserved for felines of every description.

Shortly after our wedding, we were living in a one room apartment at Seminary when a stray cat appeared on our doorstep just minutes ahead of a violent thunderstorm. We let him in. When the storm passed and we were getting ready for bed, Jeff wanted to put him out. I begged that we let him stay on our bed until he bothered us. Jeff agreed. The cat was no dummy. He stayed curled up on my side of the bed all night long and never moved a muscle. Thus, we acquired our first cat. We later learned that this particular Tom had been hanging around the married student-housing for years. He had fathered so many kittens that the seminarians took up a collection to get him neutered. Although short of the usual fee, the vet agreed to perform the surgery. Now Moshe seemed to be ours. We were warned that he wouldn't want to move with us, but we decided to try it anyway. Timing is everything. It was time for retirement apparently, and he was happy to spend the next eight or nine years with us until his death.

The next truly memorable cat was Rex. He was a Maine Coon cat who came to us as a stray. He was already neutered and the vet guessed his age at only about one year. He immediately took over the household and put our other cats in their place. It took only a little longer to train us. He enjoyed sleeping on our bed with us when we first went to sleep. But being a nocturnal creature by nature, he would wake up about 2 or 3 a.m. and demand his right to be outside. He had several creative ways of getting our attention. First, he would use his paw to open the middle door of my dresser. Then he would reach in the drawer where I kept my underwear and begin taking the pieces out one by one and dropping them on the floor. That usually got my attention. But if that failed, he would hop up on my night table and put a paw on the toggle switch which turned on the reading light over my pillow. That was guaranteed to get results. Since the only thing that would satisfy him at that point was being let outside, I would sit up, grope for my slippers, and proceed down the stairs to the door at the bottom.

So when we built our own home we designed it with a cat door where the cats could let themselves in and out, day or night. We also put a buffer of two doors that we could shut between our bedroom and the rest of the house where the cats were. No more cats in the bedroom and no more getting up at all hours to let them out.

When we moved to the Convent, we were able to install a cat door in a basement window. By this time we had two male (neutered) cats in their prime who were excellent hunters. Dugal and Digby began bringing us presents on a regular basis. They were not allowed in the bedroom, so they never brought them upstairs. But in the morning, we never knew what we might find under the piano or the dining room table. At first, it was dead mice. Then occasionally a bird. Once they were sure we understood about hunting, they decided it was time to teach us. So they would bring in a live mouse while we were reading and drop it at our feet. Of course, it would scurry away and the chase was on. The poor things would find places to hide and it would keep the cats amused for hours waiting for them to come out from hiding. When it was possible, we would catch the mouse and return it to the woods (only to be caught again?).

It was always Jeff's job to clean up the "presents" or try to catch the live critters they brought in. After all, isn't that what men are for? If it happened when Jeff was out, I would wait for him to return to clean it up. We didn't always find them all. When I had friends help remove the sofa in the living room so the hospital bed for Jeff could be set up, we found a dead mouse under the sofa.

After I became a widow, the cats carried on as usual at first. Only now I had to learn how to stop being so squeamish and clean up after them myself. Not fun. Then they decided to branch out one day: they brought in a small snake. Luckily it curled up, making a small circle so I was able to plop a plastic container over it, slide a cardboard under it and return it to the outdoors.

Next, Dugal and Digby decided on a catch and release program. They would catch a mouse or chipmunk and bring it in and release it. Then they lost all interest and it was my problem to try to catch it. They apparently realized that I wasn't doing too well in my hunting lessons so they would have to force the issue. By the time I realized what was going on I had at least one mouse who was making a good living in my kitchen. For several months, I almost always had a "have-a-heart" trap set in the kitchen. The day that I moved out of that house, I knew there was a live chipmunk running around that no one was able to catch.

All this gave me pause when I moved to my current house. The cats have had their cat door privileges revoked. They can go in or out when I open a door and let them. If they show up with something in their mouth they are not let in. So we've come full circle. They tend to go out at night. Digby learned very quickly where my bedroom window is. He usually wants in before it gets light out, so he meows under my window until I get up and open the door. Yes, cats do a very good job of training us. But I still love the furry creatures!

Windows

When I bought my house after Jeff died, I quickly discovered that the windows were in bad shape. Most of the screens were missing. Many had been painted shut and never opened after that – whenever that was. Some didn't even close properly. When I came into a bit of cash after my mother-in-law died, I decided to use some of it to get new windows.

The living room and dining room seemed ok for now, so those I didn't worry about. The previous owner had left the drapes and the sheer curtains in the living room at my request. The sheers seemed a rather dirty off-white color, but I had too many other things to think about at first. And taking them down would be a two-person job. So the next summer when my friend, Claire, came from Long Island for a visit, she agreed to help me with them. When we got them down, we could see how filthy they were, so we put them in the washer. Then we realized how dirty the windows were. You know you have a true friend when she suggests that she help clean your dirty windows. We even had to scrape splattered paint off the outside!

With a few hours of work, it was amazing how clean the windows were. The curtains turned out to be a bright white once they were laundered. When we hung them back up against the clean windows, it was remarkable how much more light came through.

As I reflected on the experience, I thought of the child who, looking at the stained-glass windows in a church, declared that saints are the people the light shines through. And who are the saints if not each one of us. We are called to let the light of Christ shine through us. But so often the light is blocked with the dirt and grime (sin) that collects on our souls. Others look at us and see only a faint light, if any at all. So how do we get rid of all the dirt. We know that confession (whether directly to God or through the discipline of sharing with a priest) is the way to let Jesus cleanse us. So washing the windows on my home was a good reminder to not let the sin accumulate on my soul.

I want to be one of those people through whom the Light of God shines. With His help, I can be.

Retreat

About 16 months after the death of my husband, I decided to make a retreat. Although I had been in the habit of yearly retreats prior to Jeff's death, I had not actually done so in several years (due to our move, his sickness, etc.). Several friends had mentioned "Emery House" to me. It is the country retreat facility of the Society of St. John the Evangelist. I made the arrangements and drove up on a Monday to begin my week of silence and being available to God.

For many people, the idea of having so much time to fill is daunting. And silence. It would drive them crazy, they think. My answer would be, first off, that most people should go on a directed retreat where there is a leader who will give mediations on a given topic. You may be given "homework" assignments for the silent periods between talks or books may be suggested for further reading. The structure gives focus to your time with God. Retreats are often given in locations where there is much natural beauty and you will have the opportunity to take walks or sit on a deck and enjoy the outdoors as you contemplate the Creator of all things.

Since such retreats are given over a weekend, when most people are free to attend, I am not able to participate due to my Sunday ministry. (My husband gave many such retreats during the two years he was at St. Mary's Convent and I have the tapes of the meditations he gave.) So I have been in the habit of making my own retreat. I always participate fully in the daily Offices and Eucharist of the community where I go. The rest of the time is spent in prayer, reading, contemplation, and sometimes writing about what I am experiencing. Weather permitting, I also like to take a long walk each day. My spiritual director (or my husband in years past) will usually suggest some reading or a direction for my thinking. Sometimes I have a particular "problem" that seems to loom large and I need to sort it out with the Lord's help.

This was true when, after 24 years on Long Island, we became convinced that it was time for my husband to seek a change. We looked all over the country and my husband interviewed at parishes in Washington, Colorado, Illinois, and upstate New York. He was on the short list for several when, out of the blue, Mother Miriam from the Community of St. Mary in Peekskill, New York, asked if he would consider coming to them as chaplain and director of their Spiritual Life Center. I was appalled! Although I had gone there for my yearly retreats for many years, I had absolutely no interest in moving there. As time went on, it became obvious that this was exactly the position that was perfect for my husband and the one that really attracted him. Now what?!

I wrestled with the Lord and cried out my misgivings. I wanted to go to Colorado or one of the other places we had been, not Peekskill! But the more I prayed and the more I tried to surrender my will and listen to what God was asking, the more I became convinced that this was where God could best use Jeff. So I agreed, reluctantly, that if that was where God was calling Jeff then there must be something there for me too, although I couldn't begin to imagine it. I felt like I was throwing my professional life down the tubes. But I knew that I had to put my feelings on hold. Jeff was being called by God to the

Community of St. Mary. Jeff and I were as close as any married couple could possibly be – spiritually and every other way. Therefore, God must be calling me too, even though I couldn't hear it or see any positive consequences. So strictly on faith, I gave my consent and we began to pack for the move.

Now, three and a half years later, I can see the hand of God so clearly in that move. He had a wonderful job for me at the parish I now serve. He made sure I was with a loving Christian community which gave my husband great comfort before he died. And as I look ahead I find it easier to believe that God will continue to take care of me.

So for this retreat, there are no big issues – just a desire to spend time apart with God. Yes, I could do it at home to some degree. But there are always distractions at home: the phone rings, you remember that the laundry really needs doing and it will only take a moment to start the machine, or that bill that came last week really has to go out in today's mail. Even if those things could be controlled, you still have to cook and clean up.

When on retreat, you have no responsibilities other than attending to God. Delicious meals are put before you three times a day, snacks are available, and you don't even help with the dishes. Your primary job – in fact your ONLY responsibility – is to be open to God. Not every retreat will end with some great revelation. But every attempt to make yourself more available to God will be used by Him for His greater glory, whether you are aware of it or not.

Camping

The urge is constant: go camping this summer. It is irresistible. I've always loved the out-of-doors and our month of camping each summer was always therapeutic: both emotionally and spiritually. Two years ago, after returning from visiting our son in Japan, we spent the rest of our vacation at Fish Creek Campground in the Adirondack Park of New York – a perennial favorite.

Of course, the purists would say that once we left our tent behind and began using first a pop-up trailer, then a slide-in truck camper, and finally a fifth wheel, we were no longer camping. And they have a valid point. When you have running water (hot and cold) and electric lights, not to mention a stove, refrigerator, and heater inside your vehicle you are, in many ways, no longer camping. But we always kept our hand in the real thing through our two-weeklong canoe trips which occurred at least every other year. At those times it was "real" camping. We slept in a tent, boiled lake water for drinking and cooking, went to bed when the sun set or sat around a campfire talking. When you have to portage every item you take for 10–14 days, you learn how much you can do without.

So now I'm back to "real" camping. I can take more than fits in a canoe since I have a small car, but I will still have no electricity or running water. I'll get the water from a spigot about 400 feet from the campsite. Flush toilets are 300 feet away and lukewarm showers are available for 25 cents about two miles down the road.

Instead of having to haul our food pack into a tree at night to keep it away from bears, I can put it in the trunk of my car. I have a small gas grill/stove for cooking and a cooler to keep food cool and fresh. So it is a step up from our canoe camping. But it is a big step down from our various campers, all of which gave us some place to go and sit comfortably on a rainy day.

A six-hour drive gets me to Fish Creek. We've had a very rainy summer and I am concerned about the weather. With a lot of rain, tent camping can be miserable. I have driven through some rain just to get here so I'm a bit apprehensive. But I arrive at my campsite on the creek with no precipitation at the moment.

Like any good camper, the first thing I do is set up the tent and put my sleeping pad, sleeping bag, and clothes inside to be sure I have at least one place to flee in case of rain. Since we have a small extra tent, I set it up too. It can act as a storage area for my pack, life jacket, lawn chair, tool kit, etc. (No food EVER in any tent.)

So far, so good. But the sky looks very unsettled, so I keep my raincoat close at hand.

Next the canoe needs to come off the car roof. I can do it by myself, but it's infinitely easier and more graceful with help. So when an older gentleman in the next campsite sees what I'm doing and offers help I accept.

The last major item for setting up camp is the screen house. It doesn't really provide much rain protection, but it's better than standing outside trying to cook in the rain. My neighbor again offers help, which I gratefully accept. As I drive the last stake in the ground, I feel the first rain drops.

After getting up early, driving six hours and setting up camp, I'm ready for a break. So I crawl into my tent, stretch out on the sleeping pad, and listen to the patter of a light rain on the nylon tent.

It lightens up after about 45 minutes, so I edge out of the tent to the soggy world of camping in the rain. The forecast is for nice weather beginning tomorrow so I muddle through fixing dinner in the screen house and keep as dry as I can.

The next three days are perfect weather: lots of sun, some high clouds, no wind (important consideration when canoeing), and temperatures in the high 70s. I canoe our favorite loop that starts right from my campsite. It includes a quarter-mile portage between lakes. I praise God for Matt's ultra-light (32 lbs.) solo canoe I'm using. Even so it takes several false starts to get this 17-foot hat correctly positioned on the hooks attached to my backpack for this purpose. (It transfers the weight to the hip belt so my neck and shoulders aren't involved.) I huff and puff my way down the trail and am inordinately proud that I managed to do this. Portaging a canoe will never be a favorite pass time, but it's good to know I can do a short one occasionally. It greatly increases the trips I can take.

Another day I take a short hike (five miles) – a new one to me. I end up at a beautiful pond with lots of lovely sitting rocks and picnic spots. About a dozen others are scattered along the shore or swimming in the clear water. Is this paradise?

By the fourth day I know, it's time to stop "doing" and spend more time "being." I have books to read, writing I want to do, and most importantly, stare into space and commune with God. It's time to string the hammock, watch the ducks that swim back and forth in front of my campsite, and listen to the occasional loon flying overhead, calling to its mate. Let the real relaxing begin.

Riding the Waves

"...breast the waves, whether sweet or bitter, looking not at them, but through them on and up to God, our Peace" (Baron F. von Hügel, *Letters to a Niece*, p. 48). That strikes me as exceptionally good advice for any widow or widower. The waves will come – waves of loneliness and fear, waves of grief or even despair – waves you didn't ask for and can't control.

I prefer to canoe in lakes and streams where motorboats aren't allowed. But sometimes I do have to share a lake with power boats. They make lots of waves and if they come fast and close, you have to take action. If you ignore the wave coming at you and it hits you broadside, a canoe can easily capsize. But if you see it approaching and turn your canoe to face the wave, chances are you can ride out even a pretty big one. That's true, of course, even if the rough water is caused by a strong wind. When your instinct says flee, your best bet is to face it head on and go through it. Once I'm pointed in the right direction, there is no point in looking at each wave. Now it helps to focus on the calmer water beyond the waves or on the distant shore.

Isn't that what von Hügel is trying to tell us? We are always better off facing the grief or loneliness. Then look beyond it and seek God who will surely be waiting for you. Only in Him will we finally be able to make it through (not around) the waves to the calm that awaits us in God's presence.

The Green Gene

Something in me demands the presence of trees and woods and preferably lakes and mountains as well. Each summer when we arrived in the Adirondacks and took our first paddle down the stream, I felt that I was inhaling something far more than the mountain air. With every breath I was breathing in God in some mysterious way. My eyes were feasting on the water, the lily pads, the coniferous forest, and my ears were relishing the quiet of nature broken only by the whispering of the wind or the whoosh of the wings of the great blue heron flying by. As I drank all this in, I felt that my soul was refreshed.

Trying to explain the spiritual significance of this to my spiritual director caused her to nod knowingly. "You have the green gene," she told me. It seems there are many of us who find it a necessity to spend time outside in God's wondrous creation.

So now at Fish creek, I'm sitting by my tent looking out over the creek. This is the last campsite on this side of the stream before it turns into wilderness. So I have an unobstructed view of birches, and pines shimmering their reflection in the water. Beyond, I see the sky and clouds. Closer to home, a chipmunk scurries past, hoping I've dropped some crumbs for his supper. A squirrel complains loudly about the intruder in his territory.

I've never seen bears at this campground, but I know they exist and since I'm camped at the last site before wilderness, I'm extra careful about food and odors. My neighbor three sites down was not as cautious. Two days ago, he was visited by a black bear at 5:30 in the morning. The bruin made off with some bread and muffins. I don't mind bears coming around but I'm unhappy to hear that he got human food. That will encourage him to come back. I didn't sleep quite as well that night.

Things That Go Bump in the Night

If you do much camping, especially wilderness camping, sooner or later you run into bears. Over the years, we've had our share of experiences that result in some fun stories for our non-camping friends who are usually horrified. Looking back, a common link has often been bacon. Bears have a keen sense of smell and bacon is obviously among their top ten favorites.

On a canoe trip in Algonquin Park, we once took some pre-cooked bacon. We wrapped it in foil and heated it over our one burner cook stove. It wasn't long before we spotted a bear on a log crossing the inlet near our campsite, heading in our direction. We shouted, threw some stones in his general direction and called his mother names. He debated for a few moments before deciding maybe we weren't such friendly dinner hosts after all.

Another time we had an encounter with a less happy ending for the bear. This black bear came to camp in the daytime. When we made noise, he looked unconcerned. When Jeff picked up stones and threw them, he got just out of reach but stayed close to camp, coming back from different directions to see how close he could get. This was not a bear afraid of humans as most are. Then I remembered the strange punctures I had found earlier that morning on the toilet paper at the outhouse. Now I made the connection: bite marks from a bear. We had already spent one night at this campsite (where we had eaten some bacon for dinner) and had planned on another before moving on. However, a bear that won't scare away in broad daylight and leaves bite marks on toilet paper is not a normal wild bear. So we hurriedly pack up our things (Jeff stands guard while I'm in the tent) and canoe to another site. Eight days later when we come out of the wilderness, we file a report about this bear. Then we learn he had become such a nuisance, no doubt having gotten human food and wanting more, that Park authorities had to go in and kill him. What a shame. It was people letting him get people food that killed him.

Tonight, I'm sitting by my campfire writing about bears, having had one more experience, although not quite directly. As I was walking back to my isolated campsite after attending a program in the amphitheater, I heard excited talking in the last occupied campsite before mine. When I heard the word bear, I called out to see what was going on. They informed me the bear had been there only moments before. They were eating a late dinner (after dark) and the bear invited himself. He didn't scare easily but throwing firewood at him had eventually done the trick.

I wasn't any too keen on continuing the walk to my deserted campsite. It was up over a hill and out of sight and sound of this last occupied site. We debated what I should do, and the camper gave me a ride to my site. After making sure the bear wasn't there I got in my car and drove to the Ranger station. I had a long talk with a man who assured me what I basically already knew: there has never been an unprovoked attack by a black bear on a human in New York state. They want food and if I keep a clean camp with *all* food in the car, I will be fine. He even told me to put my dirty clothes in the car so no cooking odors would be in the tent. That, and putting my deodorant in the car, are about the only things I can think of to do that I haven't already done. I did find the talk somewhat reassuring. I hope my brain thinks so when I stop writing, douse the fire, put the lantern out, and climb into the tent. "Have a good night," the Ranger said.

It reminded me of a medieval prayer that used to hang in our son's bedroom when he was small.

From Ghosties and Ghoulies
And long-legged Beasties
And things that go bump in the night
Good Lord, deliver us.

Amen!

Trust

Why, after 45 years as an active Christian, do I have so much trouble with trust? And I mean specifically trust in God – confidence that He will see me through, be there for me, help me, carry me when needed. I've experienced His faithfulness and goodness so many times and in so many ways.

When I was a graduate student in Germany and needed breast surgery for a cyst, He was right there. I had such an incredible peace going into that operation. When Jeff and I were first married and didn't have two nickels to rub together, I had a firm belief that He would help us. I was putting Jeff through his last year of seminary when I was laid off right before Christmas. We agonized about tithing that last check but felt God telling us He would be faithful if we were. So we gave our usual 10% to the work of the Lord and God came through for us.

Even as a well-established priest with a good salary, we had monetary worries from time to time as nearly all couples do. We would pray about any decisions that had to be made and trust God to see us through once we had done all we could. He never once let us down.

As a new widow trying to come up with a budget, I was again faced with the issue of trust. If I tithed my now lower income, I would be substantially short of balancing my budget. But I knew I wanted to be faithful, so I told God of my intention to continue my tithe and asked for His help in making ends meet. He came through with the extra service at my church and the extra salary that balanced my budget.

So why does each new twist in my budget cause such anxiety? I found out today, for instance, that my health insurance will go up 14% (almost $600!) and my out-of-pocket expenses for doctor visits will double. Ouch! So that has put me in a tailspin. I've just almost figured out how to balance my budget after the loss of the income from Sunday evening, which starts next year. Now this. Maybe I shouldn't live in the Northeast. Everything is so expensive here. But I've lived here all my life (almost) and don't have any connections to any other part of the country. My son's time in Texas will be over in 2 years and they hope to come back to the Northeast.

I've asked the Lord to help me with this issue of trust. I often pray, "Lord, help me to trust you more". Maybe that's the problem. With a prayer like that, how will I learn unless He gives me more opportunities to practice? So here I am with my mind saying one thing (of course I trust God to see me through) and my emotions another (what if I really can't make ends meet, where will I cut?).

Yesterday for Evening Prayer, the Psalms appointed were Psalm 23 and 27. "The Lord is my shepherd, I shall not be in want" (Ps. 23:1). Ok, Lord, I admit I'm like a lost sheep and you are my shepherd. If I follow you, I have your promise that I will not be in want. "The Lord is my light and my salvation; whom then shall I fear? The Lord is the strength of my life; of whom then shall I be afraid?" (Ps. 27:1). Why *am* I so fearful? Is it because I don't want to lose control? I want to have all the answers before I trust God. But in that case, where would the reliance be: on God or on me?

The Psalmist continues: "For in the day of trouble He shall keep me safe in His shelter; He shall hide me in the secrecy of His dwelling and set me high upon a rock" (vs.7). "O tarry and await the Lord's pleasure; be strong, and He shall comfort your heart; wait patiently for the Lord" (vs. 18). Clearly, I have much to learn about waiting patiently!

The choir anthem in church today was from Mendelssohn's Oratorio *Elijah*. The text is one I need to internalize.

> *Cast thy burden upon the Lord and He will sustain thee.*
> *He never will suffer the righteous to fall. He is at thy right hand.*
> *Thy mercy, Lord, is great and far above the heavens.*
> *Let none be made ashamed that wait upon Thee!*

And just to make sure I get the point, the Collect (prayer) for the day reads:

> *Grant us, Lord, <u>not to be anxious about earthly things</u>, but to love things heavenly; and even now, while we are placed among things that are passing away, to hold fast to those that shall endure; through Jesus Christ our Lord, who lives and reigns with you and the Holy Spirit, one God, for ever and ever. Amen.*

Sacrifice

As parents, we are all familiar with the idea of putting our children's needs and even wants before our own. This kind of sacrifice comes naturally to most of us because of the great love we have for our sons and daughters. In fact, giving up our own desires for those of a spouse are at the heart of marriage.

The idea of sacrifice is found throughout the Bible. In the Old Testament, we have the sacrificial system that revolves around the Temple worship. And even before that, God seals His covenant with Abraham through a sacrifice (Genesis 15:7-19). In the New Testament, we find the atonement of our sins through the sacrifice of Jesus on the cross. And then we get to Paul in the letter to the Romans. In the 12th chapter, he begins this way: "Therefore, I urge you, brothers, in view of God's mercy, to offer your bodies as living sacrifices, holy and pleasing to God – this is your spiritual act of worship."

I've always been attracted to this verse because of my desire to give myself to God. But how exactly do I do it? And what does it mean to be a living sacrifice. If I imagine an altar and try to see myself on it, one of the first things I realize is that I'm scared. (Have you ever wondered how Isaac felt when Abraham was ready to sacrifice him and he lay bound on the altar?) I don't know what will happen on the altar. I've totally lost control. So the temptation is to jump off. It seems to me that is the problem with a LIVING sacrifice. It wants to leap off the altar! But God is clear that He wants a living sacrifice, not a dead one. Paul says that we are to offer ourselves. A body is a very concrete thing. God doesn't just want our intellects; he wants ALL of us:

our minds, our souls, *and* our bodies. And the way to seal any covenant is with sacrifice.

The story of Abraham and Isaac is one that has often seemed to replay itself in my life. I find myself in a situation where God is asking a sacrifice of me. And the scary part is that I don't know if a ram is caught in the thicket or not. If I say yes to God, I may indeed have to carry through with the sacrifice. But the only way to know is to say yes and mean it. Then wait and see if He requires it.

Looking back in my journal, I find a record of such a time during Jeff's illness. Almost exactly three months before his death, I wrote: "It is rather amazing that I once again find myself in an Abraham and Isaac situation. I feel that I have to offer Jeff on the altar to God and I must do it completely. Only then, in time, will I find out if God intends to accept the offering soon (as in Jeff not living very long) or if He will provide the ram Himself and Jeff will be given a new lease on life. But the important thing is my offering, not the outcome."

More recently I've offered God my body through the offering of my hands, which, as a musician, is the way I praise and glorify God and help others to do so. Since my husband's death, I have developed a bit of arthritis in my hands, which became quite worrisome to me. After tests and doctor visits the conclusion was that no one knows if or when it will get worse or possibly stop me from playing in the future. It had me very concerned. One night as I lay in bed praying and not yet asleep, I had a "vision" in which I walked up to the altar at Zion Church and placed my hands, palms up in a gesture of surrender, on the altar. When I did so, I heard God say to me: "These are the hands that are consecrated to me, so you don't have to worry about them." Wow. So what has changed? Nothing and everything. God didn't promise to heal my hands or even to allow me to continue to play the organ (although so far that is not an issue). What He did say was not to worry. I have found it impossible to agonize about the situation the way I did before. I have offered my body to God and He has accepted that sacrifice – whatever it may mean for the future. I have His promise from Isaiah 49:16. "See, I have engraved you on the palms of my hands." With a pledge like that, I can feel secure.

The Flute

I've just spent an hour with a new parishioner who is a flute player. We had a jam session and chose some music to use in church in a few weeks. It was a fun time for both of us. But just after she left, I dissolved in tears. I didn't just cry; I sobbed. I bawled. Jeff has been gone now for a year and a half. Why this reaction? It didn't take long to put my finger on it. I probably should have expected it.

Jeff was a very good amateur flutist. In fact, that is how we met. I saw him carrying a flute case around the seminary when I was looking for a flutist for a program I would be doing on Palm Sunday at my church in New Jersey. So I asked if he would be interested in playing. I explained that I couldn't pay him, but his bus fare would be covered (by me). He jumped at the chance, always eager to get involved in music.

On our two-hour bus ride back to the city, I told him of my plans to attend a concert the following evening. When he found out I had no date, he asked if I'd like to go to dinner first. So we had our first date on Monday of Holy Week with dinner at a little German restaurant and then the St. John Passion of J. S. Bach. He loved to tell people in later years that our relationship started with passion!

Throughout the years, we often played flute and harpsichord or organ duets. We gave several parish concerts and often played as part of a benefit for one cause or another. But most of all, we played for our own enjoyment and that of our friends.

When Jeff was dying, he asked me to be sure to get a good price when I sold his flute. He didn't want it sitting on a shelf somewhere. It was too good for that. He wanted it used. So shortly after his death I contacted a flute teacher who had a student who might be interested. I drove to the student's house with the flute and met the teacher there. When I pulled into the driveway, I immediately noticed the license plate on the teacher's car: Syrinx. That is the name of a solo flute piece by Debussy that was probably Jeff's very favorite piece. That was certainly a good sign.

The student turned out to be a young Japanese girl. The teacher put Jeff's flute together and handed it to the girl asking her to play a particular Bach piece, which she did from memory. Then the teacher began playing as well and the mother and I listened to a beautiful Bach duet. I was so pleased when they bought the instrument on the spot. I knew it was what Jeff would have wanted. His instrument, which had been such a wonderful companion to him for over 40 years, was still singing.

The last time Jeff ever played in public was at Zion Church, just a few months before his death. I was doing an Evensong service with my choir and we transported the harpsichord so we could use it with the flute for the Prelude and Postlude. It was a time when the chemo had Jeff feeling very sick and he almost didn't make it through the service. But, somehow, he did and it was well done as always.

Thinking back on all of this makes it obvious why tonight was so hard. This is the first time I have accompanied a flutist since his death. And we were even playing from some of his music which I had kept. I have been a widow for 18 months now and thought I was past this kind of gut-wrenching wailing. But this was at the heart of our relationship. No wonder it hit me so hard!

Abandoned – Again

Widows quickly learn what it feels like to be abandoned. We know our husbands didn't chose to die when they did, but we nevertheless feel forsaken. As we begin our "recovery" we learn that there are others who care about us and for us and we learn to transfer some of our emotional needs to them. And I don't mean anything very concrete. At least for me it wasn't that I needed to be with them or see them frequently. It was enough to know that certain people cared enough that if I ever really needed to call on them, they would be there.

One of those people was Fr. Jim and his wife Chris. As I have already explained, he died suddenly a year after my husband, leaving me to try to be there for Chris and help her in any way I could.

Another person who is very important to me, although he probably doesn't even know it, is Fr. Miller, the priest I work for. Not only did he go through Jeff's death with me, but he told me that he felt a special obligation to be there for *me*. As a clergy spouse he was concerned about my welfare and mentioned several times that I could call him any time, day or night. Of course, I had no intention of doing so, but it was a great comfort to know that he and his wife were there in an emergency. We also get along so well on the job that several times he mentioned that he really hopes I will stay until he retires. Since we are the same age, that, too, is a great comfort. It means job security for me.

Just this last Sunday he called me into his office after church to tell me that he is leaving to take a parish in Missouri! Talk about shock!! There are many reasons for his move and all of them good ones for him. But what about me? By the time I got home, I was crying copiously. Within a period of 18 months, I was being abandoned for the THIRD time! And I felt betrayed as well. Clearly my head (it's ok) and my heart (this is horrible) were a long way apart. I have spent the last week trying to bring them together. I have been only marginally successful. Although I'm not crying at home as much, I'm still having a very hard time.

Will we get another really good priest? Will he (or she) have a deep faith and know how to communicate it? Will we be able to work well together? I know there will never be another priest who will feel the same commitment to my welfare. This was a very special pledge which gave me a sense of security in my widowhood. Now that will be gone and can never be replaced. So it's a very real loss.

I am certainly outside my comfort zone – way outside of it! So is God answering my prayer to help me learn to trust Him more? If this is what learning to trust God feels like, no wonder so few people ever try it! It's not for the faint of heart. Are you trying to tell me, Lord, that I have to trust ONLY in you? Can't I have a little help from some human friends? I don't have the strength to go it alone. Lord, have mercy.

Widows in Scripture

I was vaguely aware before my husband's death that widows are mentioned in the Bible. But after becoming a widow I suddenly realized that there are dozens of passages in both the Old and New Testaments that talk about us. Now these texts took on new meaning for me.

In the middle of Psalm 68 (v. 5), where we have been told to sing praises to God, the writer expands on the many ways in which God cares for us: "A father to the fatherless, a defender of widows, is God in His holy dwelling." And in the book of James, we are told: "Religion that God our Father accepts as pure and faultless is this: to look after orphans and widows in their distress and to keep oneself from being polluted by the world." God is telling us that we can trust Him. He will look after us and has commanded others to do so too.

In Psalm 146 (v. 9), the Lord again assures us: "The Lord watches over the alien and sustains the fatherless and the widow, but He frustrates the ways of the wicked." And in the first chapter of Isaiah, He tells the people to "Seek justice, encourage the oppressed. Defend the cause of the fatherless, plead the case of the widow." Clearly, we are an important priority to God! Wow!

In Bible times, widows were on the bottom of the social heap. Unless they had a male relative who took pity on them, they were often in very dire circumstances. Unscrupulous people took advantage of them. Hence, God's concern that they be properly taken care of. And it is interesting to note that these women who had no standing in society are often held up as examples for us!

In the story of Elijah, during the drought, he is instructed to go to a widow in Sidon and ask her for food. She is getting ready to cook her very last meal so she and her son can die. Yet when the man of God asks her to bring him something first and her supply of oil and flour will not run out, she steps out in faith to do it. And she is rewarded in the way Elijah had foretold. What a wonderful example of trust.

Another powerless widow is held up as a model of faith. This story is in the 12th chapter of Mark's Gospel. Here Jesus is watching people put money in the Temple treasury. He watches lots of rich people put in large sums out of their abundance. Then a poor widow puts in two small copper coins which have almost no value. But Jesus holds her up as an example of who we should emulate. She gave all she had. Even though the monetary value was negligible, she demonstrated her great faith in a way the others failed to do.

I find all of this most encouraging. As widows, God cares deeply about us and our situation. And we have the opportunity to be faithful witnesses even to those who may seem to have much more in life than we do. I would almost go so far as to say that since we are widows, we are in a better position to serve God than some others who have to spend time and energy (and resources) tending to the needs of their husbands. We have a unique opportunity to get close to God. Let's make the most of it.

Thanksgiving – A Year Later

What a difference a year can make! Last year at this time, I was feeling sorry for myself and having a real emotional struggle at the first major holiday since Jeff's death. This year, I was able to plan ahead. I found that our assistant priest (a woman) was also looking for someone to share Thanksgiving with. We both enjoy cooking, so we decided to team up and invite anyone else we could think of who needed a place to go. Although we asked over a dozen people, most had places to go. We ended up with 4 of us celebrating together at my house. We had a great time. I enjoyed being able to play hostess again and doing much of the cooking. My son called from Colorado where he and his wife had gone to be with friends. And even my brother-in-law called to say hi. It has been a good day.

This morning at church, I was looking through our Prayer Book and found a prayer of Thanksgiving near the back of the book that I hadn't remembered seeing before. In the midst of thanking God for His wonderful creation and the blessings of family and friends, there is this sentence:

> *We thank you also for those disappointments and failures that lead us to acknowledge our dependence on you alone.*

Oh my. I've had quite a few of those disappointments in the last 18 months. Can I really say thank you for those? Well, they *have* brought home to me just how dependent I am on God. As one "prop" after another has been taken away, I am constantly confronted with the fact that only God can be counted on. Only God is always there for me no matter what. Friends can tell me they will always be there for me and I know they mean well. They have the best intentions. But circumstances change, people become ill, they move away, they aren't available when you need them. But God is always there and always ready to listen. So even though it's a hard lesson, I am learning, sometimes reluctantly, that I must depend on God alone. I know that God works through my family and friends and I often see His face in them. But I have to be clear that they are not God and I need to be willing to let go of them at any time. I get the feeling that this will take a lifetime to accomplish and then only by the grace of God.

A Blizzard

It's early December and our first snow fall is predicted. And not just a dusting. A blizzard is headed our way. The snow starts early Friday evening and continues all night. By morning it looks like a serious storm. I'm supposed to sing in a concert of the Bach Magnificat this evening. Before noon the call comes that the concert is canceled. In fact, everything is canceled. My only concern now is being ready for tomorrow. We are doing Advent Lessons and Carols at church with all three of my choirs participating. It is also Fr. Miller's last Sunday and a big farewell luncheon is planned. To make sure I can get out in the morning I need to keep my driveway clear today. So morning, afternoon, and evening, I run the snow blower up and down the asphalt. It's a race with the wind which keeps blowing it around and putting it back on the drive. I've done all I can for now. I'll just have to wait and see what it looks like in the morning.

I like snow. A walk in the snow is pure delight to me. The stillness is unforgettable. And the beauty of new fallen snow always enchants me. At the beginning of winter, a good snowstorm brings out the nesting instinct in me. I like to make some soup and curl up with a good book. I watch the progress of the storm through the large glass doors that lead out to my deck. For some extra coziness, I turn on my propane fireplace.

This could be a lonely time, but for some reason it isn't. At least not today. The silence reminds me that I have a whole day that is pure gift. Most of the things I thought I would be doing, I can't. So what would I like to do instead. I begin by praying

Morning Prayer as I always do. But today I don't feel any pressure to be done at a certain time. I take more time with the intercessions. I let my mind think through the Scripture readings. I think back to one of the references in the Bible to snow. "Though your sins are like scarlet, they shall be as white as snow; though they are red as crimson, they shall be like wool." What a great comfort that passage is. I look at the snow outside and realize that it is covering up lots of dirt and leaves. But all I see is the pure white of the snow. When we confess our sins, they are covered by the blood of Jesus. By a great miracle, God looks and sees us looking pure and clean.

Although I participate in the General Confession during the liturgy on Sunday and even do an examination of conscience when I pray Compline, it is not often that I am truly aware of this cleansing that occurs. The times I am most apt to be aware of the covering of my sins is when I prepare for and make an auricular confession to a priest. It's a very humbling experience, especially the first time. It's never easy, but the feeling of being set free is undeniable to me when the priest pronounces the absolution. It's like looking out on the landscape of my soul and seeing a fresh covering of snow.

I bake cookies and wrap Christmas gifts and get them ready to mail. I take care of some mending that I have procrastinated doing. But then I notice that the silence is beckoning me to prayer. It is not just the physical silence of the blizzard but more importantly the silence of my inner being that calls me to spend time in God's presence. I have nothing to say to God, just a desire to be in His presence. Distractions come and I gently push them aside. There are no particular feelings associated with this prayer time. No great insights occur. But I come away with a peaceful, contented feeling. I try to stay in a prayerful attitude as I go through the rest of my day. Several choir members call just to chat about the storm. We are all concerned about getting to church tomorrow. So far, the plows haven't done much. They seem to be waiting until the snow tapers off. There is nothing I can do to prepare that I haven't done. So it's time to leave it all in God's hands and prepare for bed. I thank God again for the beauty of this day and pray for those who will be working through the night to clean off the roads.

Advent

"Rejoice" Sunday is approaching. The third Sunday in Advent has been known as *Gaudete* Sunday because of the first word of the introit in the Roman usage. But whatever you call it, the lessons and prayers all call us either directly or indirectly to rejoice. It is the Sunday when we light the pink candle on the Advent wreath. There is something different about this day.

When I first began reading the Bible as a teenager, I was struck with this note of exultation found in the book of Philippians: "Rejoice in the Lord always. I will say it again: Rejoice! Let your gentleness be evident to all. The Lord is near. Do not be anxious about anything, but in everything, by prayer and petition, with thanksgiving, present your requests to God. And the peace of God, which transcends all understanding, will guard your hearts and your minds in Christ Jesus" (4:4–7). I can't read this passage, even when I'm feeling down, without it lifting me up beyond myself.

We are called on to think about all the ways in which God is revealed to us and to rejoice in them. It may not be possible to do this in the first weeks or even months of our widowhood. But before too long, it is a good idea to try to break out of the "down" feeling and to recognize the things for which we can still express joy. God comes to us in caring friends and family and in opportunities to serve others. We meet Him in Scripture, in prayer, and in the Sacraments. He promises to see us through the difficult times. Surely all this can help us begin to find reasons to rejoice. And to remember that it is in the Lord, not in our circumstances, that we rejoice. In fact, we don't even have to be happy to be able to rejoice. But we will need to look beyond ourselves and our circumstances.

In addition to this reading from Philippians, we have a reading from Zephaniah for this Third Sunday of Advent. It includes this wonderful verse from the 4th chapter (verse 17): "The Lord your God is with you; He is mighty to save. He will take great delight in you, He will quiet you with His love; He will rejoice over you with singing." This brings to mind the picture of a baby or a toddler who is fretting and perhaps even throwing a tantrum. Nevertheless, the mother, in this case God, takes great delight in the child (me) and, through her love and caressing, will help the child to calm down. Once the child is quiet, she will sing a song of love over the child. I find it irresistible to picture myself as that child with God singing His love song over me. Not only will I find reason to rejoice, but it will also give a glimpse of that peace which passes all understanding, which God has promised to those who love Him and seek Him. Yes, indeed. Rejoice in the Lord.

Almost Christmas

My second Christmas without Jeff is almost here. We've completed all the Sundays in Advent; the next service is Christmas Eve. Is it getting any easier? I'd have to say both yes and no. Time does ease the pain and I am able to focus more on my own life and future. But, of course, the memory of Christmases gone by will always be with me. And that, too, can be both good and bad. It makes me realize how much I have lost if I dwell on it. But I am also very grateful for the many years when we were together to celebrate.

Sacred holidays are always a bit different for the clergy family or that of a church musician. And since we were both, Christmas did have a unique character. I'm a very organized person by nature, so I was able to get most things ready well in advance. But there was no way to avoid the frantic quality of the final choir rehearsals and the actual services on Christmas Eve itself. During the twenty plus years we lived on Long Island, I played for three services on Christmas Eve, each with a different choir. So while the clergy took a breather between services I was busy warming up the choir for the next service and playing the prelude or supervising the instrumentalists. My husband's schedule included two Christmas Eve services and one on Christmas morning. So the family aspect of Christmas began around noon on Christmas Day when our obligations at our respective churches were complete.

One of the things that helps me now is having so much to prepare and do at my church in connection with Christmas Eve. And this year, on Christmas Day, I will fly to Texas to be with my son. Spending Christmas week away from home is a first for me. Our relatives and friends always had to visit us since we had too many responsibilities to be able to travel.

Then I think of that first Christmas. Mary and Joseph had no choice but to travel and hardly in the best of circumstances. They had each other, which, as any widow will tell you, makes all the difference. But then, for how many years did Mary have the comfort of a husband? No one knows for sure, but legend has it that Joseph was an older man and may have died before Jesus was full grown. In any case, we do know that Mary was a widow by the time Jesus was exercising His ministry. And when He was dying on the cross, Jesus was arranging for her to be cared for by John.

Have you ever thought of what Mary went through as a widow? Not only had she lost her husband, but her firstborn was crucified as a common criminal. Mary must have wondered if she did the right thing when she told God, "I am the Lord's servant. May it be to me as you have said." Obedience to God can be very costly. But we get no hint that she ever regretted it. If we, as widows, are looking for a role model, I would suggest that Mary is a good one. Her willingness to be obedient to whatever God asked of her gives us an example to follow. Being an unwed, pregnant teenager was no picnic in Mary's day. In fact, it usually meant death by stoning. That brings most of our problems down to size.

So this Christmas Eve, when I get to church (I'll plan to get there before all the commotion of my children's choirs arrival), I will spend some time in adoration. Not only will I thank our God for sending us His Son, Jesus. I will also bless Him for giving us the example of Mary who became a widow much too young, but went on to be part of that first Christian community and is honored throughout Christendom.

On nights like this, it often seems that the curtain between heaven and earth is more permeable than usual. That was certainly true 2,000 years ago when the shepherds saw the angels. Perhaps if I listen closely, I'll be able to hear Jeff's booming bass voice in the heavenly choir:

Gloria in excelsis Deo!

About Author

Beverly grew up in Bethesda, Maryland, as well as Germany and Austria – a total of six years abroad, plus a year of graduate study. She earned a B.A. in Music Education from the University of Oregon and a Master of Sacred Music degree from Union Seminary in New York City. It was while getting the latter degree that she met the love of her life, Jeffrey Simmons. He was ordained a priest in the Episcopal Church a year and a half after they married.

During their 31 years of marriage, they lived in Wisconsin, Illinois, and mostly on Long Island, New York. Beverly was a stay-at-home Mom, raising one son and working as a Minister of Music (organist, choirmaster) in a different parish from the one where her husband worked.

After his death, she moved to Poughkeepsie, New York, where she held two different church positions, played at a synagogue, and taught piano. After thirteen years, she "retired" and moved to Albuquerque, New Mexico. Within a year, she accepted a job as Minister of Music at her parish church where she continues to enjoy serving God through music.

Also available from Balm and Blade Publishing

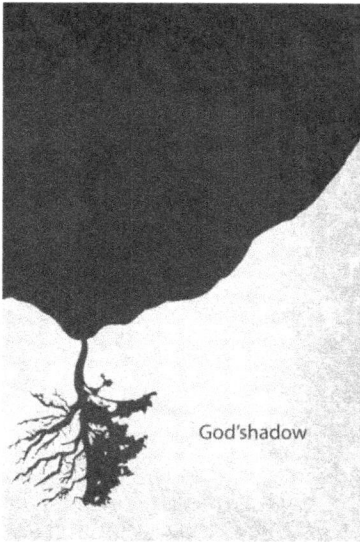

God'shadow

Daniel de Sevén takes us on journey deeper into doubt through a variety of creative essays meant to recall dormant doubts in the reader or else to create new ones. For many it will be an uncomfortable adventure but it is, the author argues, a necessary one because doubt is the delivery room of faith.

But be warned: this book isn't about the author trying to inductively prove a point. Rather, it is at once disjointed and communal, allowing readers to join the discussion and reach their own conclusions.

Revelation is the end.

It's often the end of our curiosity, at least. The people who really love Revelation often strike us as a bit… unbalanced. The complexity of the composition intimidates us. We'd rather keep the polite company of the Gospels or the superhero stories of the Old Testament.

We give up too easily.

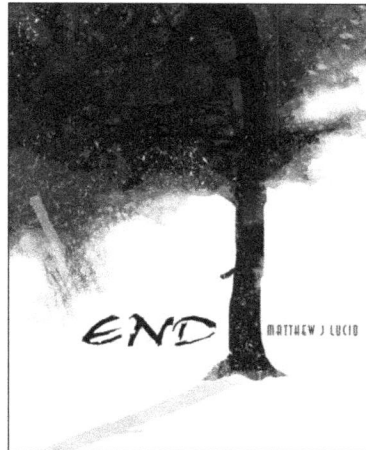

END

MATTHEW J LUCIO

This isn't a commentary. It's a set of devotional forays into the bog of the book, which are meant to show us that Revelation is worth wrestling with. There's a beauty in this mystery, terrifying and pure. Engaging Revelation unlocks a more balanced perspective on the rest of the Bible.

If you're brave enough to explore these haunted woods then you'll find that… Revelation is the beginning. (Matthew J. Lucio)

For the latest news and updates
from Balm and Blade Publishing,

please visit us at:
balmandblade.com
facebook.com/balmandblade

BALM AND BLADE
PUBLISHING

www.ingramcontent.com/pod-product-compliance
Lightning Source LLC
Chambersburg PA
CBHW051839040426
42447CB00006B/602